# SOME SPIRITUAL DANGERS

## FACING THE CHURCH

# Some Spiritual Dangers Facing The Church

R. H. McGraw

Published by Reggie McGraw Ministries, 2024.

While every precaution has been taken in the preparation of this book, the publisher assumes no responsibility for errors or omissions, or for damages resulting from the use of the information contained herein.

SOME SPIRITUAL DANGERS FACING THE CHURCH

**First edition. April 20, 2024.**

Copyright © 2024 R. H. McGraw.

ISBN: 979-8224286393

Written by R. H. McGraw.

# PREFACE

This book was written to provide the body of Christ with some insights into points of attack against believers from the kingdom of darkness. There is no pretense made that the items presented in the chapters that follow are by any means a comprehensive list of the same. Indeed, a text even approaching a delineation and exhaustive analysis of all such nefarious weapons would most assuredly produce a work rivaling an unabridged dictionary in size, and still be likely to leave out at least a few critical items. Therefore, the reader is encouraged to understand that the use of the word "some" in the book title is deliberate.

The chapter titles in this book are not to be construed as necessarily naming a particular demonic entity, but rather a concept of spiritual attack. Indeed, some chapters do identify an agent from the kingdom of darkness with a specific name, but this was limited so as to focus rather on problems they create. Consequently, the chapters that follow are designed to be a source of revelation knowledge regarding some of the "wiles of the devil." At the same time, there is presented information relevant to each subject that will expand and enlighten the reader for a broader conceptual understanding.

There is no particular pre-determined rationale for the sequence of the chapter topics. As the Lord has led this author to type in the words for each division, there was usually no directive as to what the next chapter would be until the current one was completed. In this way, the text did not flow from hour to hour, but rather often interludes of days between chapters being completed and the next one initiated. Consequently, there is no pretense of "linear flow" from division to the next, but rather a "stand alone" teaching that is founded on its own merit.

# TABLE OF CONTENTS

# CHAPTER 1
# THE MENTAL ASSENT ENEMY IS IDENTIFIED

# CHAPTER 1
# THE MENTAL ASSENT ENEMY IS IDENTIFIED

One spirit of deception that has been turned loose against the church is that of **MENTAL ASSENT.** This agent from the kingdom of darkness has deceived many of God's people, and most of whom are blissfully unaware of both its intent and even its presence. Quite commonly, the spirit of mental assent is accompanied by other demonic entities. For example, there is a very real demonic entity of **SPIRITUAL BLINDNESS.** We can find in John 12:39-40 the words:

> 39 Therefore they could not believe, because that Esaias said again

> 40 He hath blinded their eyes, and hardened their heart; that they should not see with their eyes, nor understand with their heart, and be converted, and I should heal them. (KJV)

In this passage of scripture, there is the statement that the eyes of the religious Israelites were prevented from seeing something, which here was spiritual truth. However, the verses quoted also present a revelation that many have missed: understanding of said spiritual truth was not performed by the mind, but by the "heart" of an individual. This is not to infer the blood-pumping organ of a man or woman is the center of this discussion, but rather it is the spirit-man inside each born again person that makes possible the comprehension of spiritual truths. Indeed, the Word of God declares:

12 Now we have received, not the spirit of the world, but the spirit which is of God; that we might know the things that are freely given to us of God.

13 Which things also we speak, not in the words which man's wisdom teacheth, but which the Holy Ghost teacheth; comparing spiritual things with spiritual.

14 But the natural man receiveth not the things of the Spirit of God: for they are foolishness unto him: neither can he know them, because they are spiritually discerned. (1 Cor. 2:12-14, KJV)

Herein the Lord is stating that while the Bible contains words that can be read by literate individuals, those same words carry spiritual truth that an unsaved person cannot hope to fully comprehend. Why is that? The things of the Spirit of God are such that they are on a different level of truth beyond mere words, considered foolishness, and thus merely brushed aside from any normal cognitive consideration. Still worse is the fact that many churchgoers are "natural," i.e., not born-again people, and so week after week, month after month, season after season, year after year, these persons attend church, but do not have the spiritual capacity to receive the Truth of the Word of God. Consequently, they have fallen victim to the spirit of mental assent in that while they may acknowledge what they heard in church was scriptural, their spirit-man is blind with no discernment. In other words, what they may have heard they will perhaps admit was "true," but that the information was just not appropriate or meaningful for application in their respective lives.

Jesus addressed this spirit of mental assent when He stated: "This people draweth nigh unto me with their mouth, and honoureth me with their lips; but their heart is far from me" (Matt 15:8, KJV). This hypocritical approach to God was then, and is still today, one of the characteristics of religion and religious traditions. Religion can be defined as "repetition without revelation." In other words, there are rites and rituals that are performed in a prescribed manner season after season, and going through the motions of each tradition supposedly demonstrates the religious persons' holiness and dedication to God. The problem is that the performance of these ceremonies is only an external show, while internally the spiritual heart of the individual(s) is not at all dedicated to the Lord or seeking His glory.

Jesus condemned such adherence to rituals and traditions of mental assent when He stated: "Making the word of God of none effect through your tradition, which ye have delivered: and many such like things do ye" (Mark 7:13, KJV). In the Old Testament, the Levitical priesthood stood as God's representatives through whom ordinary people of the other tribes of Israel could approach and appease the Lord as with animal sacrifices for sin, etc. The rites and rituals of temple worship became spectacles of observance performed to the letter of the law, but there was no love for God expressed in them. In fact, perhaps save for some "holy words" spoken during these priestly rituals, acknowledging God was left out, and the monotonous chores associated with the procedures became the sole object of the same. It got so far out of order, in fact, that two priests thought that they could wear their priestly garments and perform offerings to God that He had not ordained. The account of this can be found in Lev. 10:1-2.

1 Now Nadab and Abi'hu, the sons of Aaron, each took his censer, and put fire in it, and laid incense on it, and offered unholy fire before the Lord, such as he had not commanded them.

2 And fire came forth from the presence of the Lord and devoured them, and they died before the Lord. (RSV)

These two sons of Aaron were carried out of the temple and out of the camp in their "coats" (priestly garments) and buried (Lev. 10:4-5). So their holding the office of priests, their wearing of special robes reserved for the priesthood, and their offering incense to the Lord as an outward show of "holiness" were all to no avail. They died because of practicing some ritual with which they were so familiar that they apparently thought it would bring them into the presence of God. Obviously they were very wrong. One can only wonder what might occur in churches today, were it not for the mercy of the Lord, when traditions were performed as their usual outwardly religious show!

The deceitfulness and hypocrisy of mental assent, however, go far beyond mere behavioral habituation in church. Indeed, one of the very real dangers of churchgoers falling victim to mental assent is that of ending up in hell for eternity. This is spelled out in John 3:16-18:

> 16 For God so loved the world, that he gave his only begotten Son, that whosoever believeth in him should not perish, but have everlasting life.
>
> 17 For God sent not his Son into the world to condemn the world; but that the world through him might be saved.
>
> 18 He that believeth on him is not condemned: but he that believeth not is condemned already, because he hath not believed in the name of the only begotten Son of God. (John 3:16-18, KJV)

Many good, moral, and responsible persons maintain going to church as an integral part of their weekly lifestyle. While this is fine in and of itself, the point to be made is that regularly spending time in a church building can no more make anyone a Christian than does standing every night in the garage make anyone an automobile! It simply does not work that way! It makes no difference what some church with or without stained glass windows might teach its attendees to the contrary. In order to be a Christian an individual must: (1) believe in their heart (not just their head!) that Jesus is real and that He is alive; (2) believe that Jesus was crucified, dead, and was raised up alive by God; and (3) confess (say) with their own mouth these heart-established things to God. Believing teachings from the Bible with the mind (the head) is one thing, but believing the same with an unshakable conviction in one's heart (spirit-man) that these scriptural truths must be spoken back to God as an act of faith is absolutely mandatory.

The main problem with mental assent, once it has been established over a period of time regarding some doctrine or belief, is that human pride does not like to willingly admit it might be wrong and have to change opinions or beliefs. Consequently, it is locked up in the fortress of a person's head and aggressively defended. When sufficient numbers of such erroneous teachings are accumulated by large numbers of people, whole denominations can split off from main-line Biblical truth. So for instance, when churches teach their people about praying to statues of deceased religious leaders, praying to a woman, turning church buildings into restaurants sponsoring dinners to fund various efforts, and so on and so forth, the real question that should be asked is, "Where is that stated in the Bible?" For churchgoers, if the belief or activity is not supported by scripture, there is absolutely no reason to give a moment's consideration to any of it and instead completely reject it. This mental assent must be condemned such "that we henceforth be no more children, tossed to and fro, and carried about with every wind of doctrine, by the sleight of men, and cunning craftiness, whereby they lie in wait to deceive " (Eph 4:14, KJV).

As a final item of discussion concerning mental assent in the church today, one glaring example of the same needs to be included here: praise and worship music. There has been a trend for decades to provide churches with up-beat music and contemporary choruses for choirs and congregational singing that are new and expressive. The tempo and the instrumentation of said musical performances are definitely not the issue here. Rather, the words at the heart of such songs are often suspect. Indeed, some praise and worship songs provided by "reputable" tune mills that crank out hundreds, if not thousands, of choruses and songs that in many cases are simply not scriptural! Many of these lyrics are plainly directly opposed to truths from the Bible, yet the **mental assent** that exists in continuing to sing such drivel is apparently a stamp of approval because, "Well, this is a reputable gospel song provider of national recognition, and they certainly wouldn't offer anything that didn't glorify God or contradict the Bible!"

At the risk of appearing almost heretical, a few examples of unscriptural "praise and worship" lyrics will be presented. One chorus belted out in many church services includes the line: "I'm running after you, Lord!" A variation of this same thing is: "I want to be close, close by your side." Apparently neither the songwriter nor the singers of such verbiage have read Colossians 1:26-27.

> 26 Even the mystery which hath been hid from ages and from generations, but now is made manifest to his saints:

> 27 To whom God would make known what is the riches of the glory of this mystery among the Gentiles; which is Christ in you, the hope of glory: (KJV)

Add to the truth in these verses the statement in Hebrews 13:5, "Let your conversation be without covetousness; and be content with such things as ye have: for he hath said, I will never leave thee, nor forsake thee" (KJV). Since the Lord has promised to never leave us or forsake us, and indeed, He has come to dwell within us if we are born-again believers, what sort of nonsense is it to "run after" someone residing within? What sense does it make to sing about being "close by your side," when again He dwells within our spirit-man? If Christians indeed have the necessity to run after Jesus just to be "close by His side," then we have made Him out to be a plain-faced liar, (which of course He is not).

Some readers might attempt to rebuff such discussions by concluding, "Well now, brother, you are just getting off into legalism and forgetting that the letter kills but the spirit gives life. God understands what we are singing!" Oh really? So in other words, the Lord is supposed to deem as acceptable and true those lyrics that are in direct contradiction to His Word? Such "sloppy agape" can be carried out to deliberate extremes, and to demonstrate just how incorrect such mental assent can be, the following example is offered.

We can read, "But thou art holy, O thou that inhabitest the praises of Israel" (Ps 22:3, KJV). Without any qualifications or scriptural restrictions, some overly zealous songwriter could easily maintain, "Okay, so since God dwells in our praise, let's concentrate on 'praise.' Let's praise the Father, let's praise the Son, and let's praise the Holy Ghost. Let's pour out praise for the sun, the moon, the stars, the rivers, tree stumps, the weeds and the flowers since He dwells in our praise! Heck, let's continue lifting praise even for Satan, the demons, the fires of hell, and praise for the fact that he comes but for to steal, kill, and destroy!" Some readers might be repulsed by such a deliberate extreme, (and this author is definitely not advocating any such thing!), but singing songs that violate both spiritual truth and the letter of the Word of God are just as much in error as this "praise" example. If the Holy Spirit gift of discerning of spirits operated in many congregations, they would be appalled to see demon spirits in the shadows chuckling week after week at the power-less, tearjerker, and unscriptural songs performed by choirs and congregations throughout the land!

# Questions for Study and Discussion from Chapter 1

1.  What is mental assent, and why is it so difficult a problem with which to deal?
2.  Why check scriptures to verify spiritual teaching when dealing with mental assent?
3.  What are the differences between a "churchgoer" and a "born-again Christian"?
4.  Explain the relationship between religious hypocrisy and mental assent.
5.  What is the difference between "legalism" and "spiritually accurate truth"?

# Prayer for Dealing with Mental Assent

Heavenly Father, I come in Jesus' name to ask you to forgive me for clinging to any mental assent that has set up a stronghold in my mind. Your Word has declared that "...the weapons of our warfare are not carnal, but mighty through God to the pulling down of strong holds; casting down imaginations, and every high thing that exalts itself against the knowledge of God, and bringing into captivity every thought to the obedience of Christ." So in the name of Jesus, by faith I come against any unscriptural beliefs that I have maintained in the past, and I pull those things down now. Holy Spirit, thank you for leading me into the scriptural truths of Your Word to have replaced those former false teachings. As I grow in the knowledge of Your Word, Lord, thank you for continuing to prosper my mental "house cleaning" of any and all mental assent that I discover. In Jesus' Name I pray. Amen.

# CHAPTER 2
# GREVIOUS WORSHIP

The Bible admonishes us to "Let all things be done decently and in order" (1 Cor. 14:40, KJV). When it comes to the traditional sequence of events for Sunday services in many churches, this has become a ritual virtually engraved in stone. Many congregations receive a bulletin outlining the strict progression of each and every element in the morning (and sometimes also the evening) service every week. The detailed information contained in said document often includes not only the name of songs to be sung and their hymnal page number, but also the anticipated verses to be sung for each as performed by the choir and/or the congregation. Each person who steps up to the podium or who temporarily commands the microphone is identified in the bulletin, complete with their official church title. Last, but certainly not least, the understood end of the service must occur at a specified time. Woe be to the person or persons responsible for the service lasting more than a few minutes beyond its normal cutoff goal. This latter point is particularly egregious for any church gathering scheduled to end at precisely noon, as this will put the congregates at a significant disadvantage for table service at restaurants when other more punctually correct churches have already filled most available seating!

We may smile at reading an objective overview of what occurs in many churches, but the fact remains that "decently and in order" has come to mean a prescribed series of theater by various players on a stage disguised as the sanctuary platform each Sunday. In one church, a discussion within the "College and Careers" Sunday school class of said ritualistic services resulted in a written plan for a totally different trial run format on a future Sunday. This new script for the church service on Sunday morning even included one of the young men volunteering to preach the sermon so that there was "a day off" for the pastor.

The result from the submission of this trial balloon floated into the hands of church leadership? Absolutely nothing was changed, with the exception of one additional song being sung at some point where it had not been previously. (The bulletin, however, did have to be updated to accommodate the new entry into the sequence of events!)

Much more insidious is the "praise and worship" aspect of most Sunday services. First of all, the praise and worship is almost always immediately followed by the anointing-killing announcements. After the choir and congregation sing their hearts out to welcome the Holy Spirit into their midst, it is as if the leadership says to the Lord, "Hey, God, hang in there a second while we announce the baby showers (or whatever have you)!" Then when the yada yada is complete, leadership then turns their attention back to the heavens and effectively will say, "Okay, God, we've got our agenda complete, now if you will be so kind as to step back into this service, we'll go on with church today!" For the most part, Biblical order for praise and worship songs was totally absent, and often have included choruses with unscriptural concepts (see Chapter 1). The admonition of Eph. 4:30 states, "And grieve not the Holy Spirit of God, whereby ye are sealed unto the day of redemption" (KJV). Since this was written to Christians, it apparently is entirely possible to grieve the Holy Spirit through unscriptural practices, and the powerlessness of many contemporary services stands as mute testimony to His being both pushed aside and excluded by ritual and tradition. Indeed, one man stated that if the Holy Spirit were lifted from the Earth, many church services would go on just as always as if nothing had happened!

So where do we begin to eliminate grievous worship in our churches? One place to begin is that of "honesty." If the service is scheduled to begin at 9:00AM, then it is dishonest for the leadership of that congregation to start at 9:15 or later. If key personnel such as choir leaders cannot reliably be in place on time every time, then either the posted start time must be changed to eliminate the weekly lie, or a permanent personnel change must be made. One pastor took this concept to heart and simply locked the entry doors at the time church started. Late-comers got to read the signs posted on the inside of the glass doors indicating that the doors would not be unlocked until service was over! Tardiness on the part of many persons was immediately corrected. Far from being "dictatorial" on the part of leadership, grieving the Holy Spirit as He moved in the midst of the people which was formerly caused by late-comers stepping over feet, purses and coats colliding with worshipers whose hands are raised in praise to the Lord, etc. was eliminated.

Jesus admonished us to "... Render therefore unto Caesar the things which are Caesar's; and unto God the things that are God's (Matt 22:21, KJV). We all have job and family responsibilities, and many times we are distracted or just plain unaware of things of which we should be cognizant. God is not the author of confusion! Church is therefore no place for congregations to endure leadership making "announcements" from the platform that are of incorrect date, time, place, contact persons, etc. and repeatedly asking individuals seated in the auditorium for the correct data. "Let all things be done decently and in order" (1 Cor. 14:38, KJV). Replace the order of worship scorecard (bulletin) with accurate printed announcements to which congregates are directed after being greeted in gathering for the service. The weekly hubbub of activities due to "Caesar" can thus be immediately deflected decently and in order, making way for the things of God in praise and worship to have their rightful place. This greatly reduces the likelihood of grieving the Holy Spirit with confusion and delays.

Church is a place for two or more to gather and meet with God. As such two directions of ministry must be recognized: one horizontal and one vertical. As leadership calls to the people to prepare for worship, songs of horizontal ministry to the people in the auditorium should be such as to help them set aside the cares outside the church and focus on the Lord. However, when praise and worship to God begins, it is inappropriate, and therefore a source of grievous ministry to the Holy Spirit, for hit-or-miss vertical ministry, i.e., horizontal ministry repeatedly mixed in with vertical ministry. Indeed, for some song-leader's favorite tearjerker chorus to be sung repeatedly at least six to ten times about one's struggles and trials would be bad enough. However, when interjected into a sequence of vertical ministry to the Lord, it is not only out of Biblical order, but amounts to grievous ministry into the face of the Holy Spirit.

There is, in fact, a Biblical order for vertical ministry. We can find in Psalm 100:4 the words: "Enter into his gates with thanksgiving, and into his courts with praise: be thankful unto him, and bless his name" (KJV). After the call to worship, lifting heart-felt thanks to God for the things He has done, is doing, and will by faith continue to do in our lives, is where the scripture indicates we should direct our singing. Next in proper sequence is "praise." This praise flows quite naturally from a heart of thanksgiving, as Jesus is worthy of all of our praise (and then some)! Quite apart from the works of God, however, next is the recognition of who He is and His nature, as worship to Him. Worship culminates ministering to the Lord in acknowledging His holiness, His righteousness, divine sovereignty, and so on **about His nature as the only true God**. Some persons may take issue with several aspects of this Biblical order of worship, but the intent here is not to stir up controversy, but rather to lift high praise and worship to the Lord and totally avoid any grievous ministry.

There have been many occasions in which church services experienced a powerful move of God when the very first song and all subsequent singing were of worship and magnifying the Lord. This was obviously totally acceptable, with great and mighty things occurring in the remainder of those services. Indeed, in some instances, the Holy Spirit directed the leadership to forego preaching and begin ministry to those needing healing, deliverance, salvation, and so on. This is one glaring reason for eliminating the incessant play-by-play scorecard disguised as a bulletin so that the Holy Spirit can take control of the service. In no way, however, is this a call for chaos in things like lack of preparation by the choir, the ushers, the audio/video personnel, and so on. There must be order (I Cor. 14:40), but not something so rigidly enforced that the Holy Spirit is effectively pushed aside and out of the flow of the service, resulting in grievous ministry.

The sermons presented in church should likewise be subject to the governance of the Holy Spirit. Many has been the time that a pastor approached the pulpit with his prepared message, and before he could even get started, the Lord directed him into an entirely different train of thought and sermon topic. Does this mean that ministers are to step into the pulpit unprepared? No, of course not, as that would virtually guarantee grievous ministry! However, when God is in charge of the service, dynamic things can happen. R. W. Schambach was a remarkable preacher who on one occasion had his prepared sermon dramatically interrupted by the Holy Spirit. While he was yet speaking, all of the wheelchair-bound folks got up out of their chairs and spontaneously walked to the front of the church, healed, strong, and praising God! Imagine someone telling those people to go and sit back down because the sermon was not finished!

One certain minister asked the Lord if He had a favorite verse in the Bible. The Lord answered him and said, "Yes, it is Third John verse two." That particular verse states, "Beloved, I wish above all things that thou mayest prosper and be in health, even as thy soul prospereth" (3 John 2, KJV). Thus it is safe to say that God wants people to be in good health and not suffering from any infirmity or symptoms of the same. The Bible also records:

14 Is any sick among you? let him call for the elders of the church; and let them pray over him, anointing him with oil in the name of the Lord:

> 15 And the prayer of faith shall save the sick, and the Lord
> shall raise him up; and if he have committed sins, they shall
> be forgiven him. (James 5:14-15, KJV)

While we know that there is certainly no "magic" in the anointing oil used by the elders for such prayers, the point to be made is that tremendous healings do occur when these prayers with the anointing oil are performed in the name of Jesus. The difficulty arises when some churches have spectacular healing results, while other congregations rarely see any evidence of healing manifestations at all when this part of the service occurs. Why is that? A number of reasons could be offered, but one glaringly obvious cause is that of grievous ministry. You see, a consideration of Mark 16:20 will reveal one crucial bit of information.

> 20 And they went forth, and preached everywhere, the Lord
> working with them, and confirming the word with signs
> following. Amen. (Mark 16:20, KJV)

The Lord confirms His Word with signs such as divine healing. However, when leadership decides to insert an anointing ceremony into the service as some "convenient" interlude prior to the Word of God being preached, there is no obedience to Mark 16:20. Moreover, when the effort to accommodate said anointing service is made, most of the time there is no opportunity given for those needing healing to "call for the elders of the church" (3 John 2:14, above), even so much as a simple raising of one hand to indicate their need. Herein, then, is another example of grievous ministry. The anointing service is not to be performed prior to the preaching of the Word. In many churches, however, the anointing service is, in fact, done after the preaching, but the problem is that this is usually offered after the service has been dismissed. Congregates at this point often are milling around talking and walking by the platform, especially those with children in tow, who all contribute to confusion at the altar. Stated simply, this sort of unruliness grieves the Holy Spirit.

How to overcome this sort of disobedience to the Word of God and thus restore the flow of divine healing in our church services requires a few very simple adjustments. First and foremost, the anointing with oil is to be performed after the sermon is complete. Alternatively, a special section of the service prior to the sermon could have the admonitions of several scriptures on divine healing spoken to the congregation. Next, when the elders are in place at the front of the church, a simple request from the podium for those wanting to be anointed with oil for healing to "call for," or in this case merely alert, the elders of their need by raising one hand. Then, those persons who raised a hand can make their way to the front of the church and be anointed and prayed for by the assembled elders. Proper training of the ushers to facilitate this will be greatly appreciated by those needing assistance to get to the front. Elders may pray as a group or as single individuals in front of whom lines form if the number of persons coming to the front of the church is large.

The elders should, of course, inquire of the individual coming for prayer as to what specific physical need they have. A special consideration for this procedure is that wherever possible, male elders pray with men, and female elders pray with the women. The musicians and choir could assist in this ministry by singing songs appropriate for healing and deliverance, e.g., "There is power in the blood." If not already completed, the offering could be received following the anointing ministry, and the remainder of the service be concluded. Churches should be prepared for and expect dramatic manifestations of healing when such scriptural guidelines are followed.

The point to be made in avoiding grievous ministry is that our services must be in line with the scriptures, and leadership must always be ready to have the Holy Spirit shift any preplanned sequences of events. For many churches, regardless of the name over the entry door of the building, there will be no, or very few, adjustments needed to be made in this regard. However, in many other cases, wholesale restructuring of regular services will be required, and this will inevitably stir up resistance to change. Leadership of these latter bodies of believers thus will have a choice: get in line with the leading of the Holy Spirit, or continue on in business as usual with grievous ministry. There is no middle ground, although the process of making changes may require some number of services to fully implement the "new normal" of worship. We must allow the Holy Spirit to have His way and have leadership that is sensitive to the same.

Questions for Study and Discussion from Chapter 2

1) What are some ways contemporary church services grieve the Holy Spirit?

2) Explain the differences between horizontal versus vertical ministry during praise and worship.

3) What are some of the ways leadership can prevent grievous worship from occurring?

4) Identify some places where "decently and in order" could be applied to our church services.

5) What roles do the ushers have in preventing grievous worship practices?

Prayer Regarding Worship in Contemporary Services

Heavenly Father, we come to you in the Name of Jesus to obtain your wisdom and help in worshiping and praising You in our church. Forgive us for where we have missed the mark in this regard in the past.

Help us to renew our minds to the Word of God in celebrating and worshiping You and Your Love.

# CHAPTER 3
# FAULTY FUTURE FAITH

The Bible records that, "...The just shall live by faith" (Rom. 1:17; Gal. 3:11; and Heb. 10:38, KJV). Many churchgoers will immediately interject, "Well, I believe in God, therefore I have faith!" That statement is not necessarily true, since James 2:19 records, "Thou believest that there is one God; thou doest well: the devils also believe, and tremble" (KJV). So if the devils believe in God and it is not accounted to them as "faith," then perhaps merely believing in something or someone is not accurately what could be called "faith."

The classic definition of "faith" is found in Hebrews 11:1, which states, "Now faith is the substance of things hoped for, the evidence of things not seen" (KJV). Where does "faith" come from? We are informed in Romans 10:17, "So then faith cometh by hearing, and hearing by the word of God" (KJV). Thus a spiritual transaction of sorts occurs when the Word of God is heard, received, and believed such that "faith" should be formed in the spirit-man of the hearers. The Bible furthermore informs us that "faith" is not a mental quantity, but rather it is a spiritual entity: "We having the same spirit of faith, according as it is written, I believed, and therefore have I spoken; we also believe, and therefore speak" (2 Cor. 4:13, KJV). The book of Genesis records, "And God said, Let us make man in our image, after our likeness..." (Gen. 1:26, KJV). Thus since man was created as God's type of being (a spirit), coupled with 2 Cor. 4:13 just quoted, it is accurate to state that man is a speaking spirit. Interestingly, we are furthermore told the origin of our words: "...for out of the abundance of the heart the mouth speaketh" (Matt. 12:34, KJV). It is therefore easy to assess what resides predominantly within any individual simply by listening to what they say! Sadly, for many Christians, that which pours out of their mouths is not words of "faith" from the Bible.

The spiritual dynamic involved with "faith" is that "... faith without works is dead" (James 2:20, KJV). In other words, the spirit of faith must be activated and doing something, or else it becomes lifeless and therefore useless. As quoted previously, Second Corinthians 4:13 plainly declares that one manifestation of the spirit of faith is that it SPEAKS. Obviously, if a person is making statements that are opposed to, or in direct contradiction to, the Word of God, faith is not activated by such unbelief. Since the spirit of "fear" (2 Tim. 1:7) is the opposite of the spirit of "faith," then those things spoken in unbelief manifest the spirit of fear in some way, shape, or form.

Another aspect of the spiritual dynamic of "faith" is that it is always a "now" phenomenon. Without an appreciation of the fact that "faith" deals with the unseen in the present tense, however, this parameter of the spirit of faith cannot be grasped. So, for instance, we find the admonition, "Therefore I say unto you, What things soever ye desire, when ye pray, believe that ye receive them, and ye shall have them" (Mark 11:24, KJV). This statement means that our "faith" becomes embodied as the thing desired in a prayer of petition at the moment we pray, and the Word of God assures us that we will have a manifestation of the "whatsoever thing" in His timing if we continue believing His Word. Unfortunately, for many churchgoers, their "faith" puts the answer to prayers off into the future, rather than at the moment of request. This is a picture of faulty future faith. A common statement from such individuals is something to the effect, "I just know that God is going to do it." This sort of belief reflects a prayer that the Lord cannot answer because it violates His Word. We are to receive the answer at the moment we make the request, not sometime off in the near or distant future.

Faulty future faith is often the result of the carnal (natural man's) mind attempting to manipulate the principle of reaching into the unseen realm of the spirit world and getting it to manifest in the physical world. The time period of delay between the moment of asking in prayer and the moment for manifestation of the desired answer is where "faith" stands in the gap. So what are we to do during the aforesaid "gap" period of time? For many persons, the unfortunate response is, "Well if I can't see it or feel it, I'm not going to believe it." This nullifies their prayer, and they may never witness the manifestation of their prayer requests. Faulty future faith can even have fatal consequences. One dear sister was taken with a life-threatening physical condition, and her constant confession subsequent to prayer for her healing was, "I just know that God is going to heal me!" Unfortunately, she died. The point to be made is that trying to send "faith" off into the future is an exercise in futility.

A minister named Creflo Dollar once defined faith as "a positive response to what the grace of God has already done." This to say that first we recognize what the Lord has already provided for each of us according to His word. Our "positive response" to what He has accomplished is to ask in faith, then thank Him for answering our prayer with what we believe we have received before we see the answer with our natural eyes. The Bible records that in this regard we are imitating God in the way He desires by "calling those things that be not as though they already were" (see Rom. 4:17). Since "God is not a man that He should lie, nor the Son of man that He should repent..." (Num. 23:19), God is not lying by calling things that be not as though they already are, and neither are we!

An example of this application of faith can be found in the account from the wife of Dr. Bill Winston. His wife needed a job, but employment agencies were merely telling all applicants that no one was hiring at that time. She and her husband sat down and made a list of the things desired in a job for her, including a close proximity to home and the salary needed. They agreed together in prayer on scriptures such as "But my God shall supply all your need according to his riches in glory by Christ Jesus" (Phil 4:19, KJV), and thanked Him for her new job. When a friend dropped by for a visit within a few days, the question was asked if she had found a job yet. The response was "Yes!" When asked where it was and what she work she would be performing, her reply was, "I don't know where my job is yet or what I will be doing, but I definitely have a new job." Within a short period of time, she got a call for a job interview at a position very near her house with a salary that exceeded her expectations. Coincidence? No, but she and her husband kept their faith in the present tense ("now") and did not succumb to faulty future faith. This, then, exemplifies the sort of thing we are to do in the gap period between the moment of prayer and the moment of manifestation, namely to continue making a positive response with thanksgiving for what God has already done for us.

The Bible records, "According as his divine power hath given unto us all things that pertain unto life and godliness, through the knowledge of him that hath called us to glory and virtue" (2 Peter 1:3, KJV). The verb form "hath given" is in the past perfect tense. In other words, it refers to things already done. This has led some to describe use of "faith" as accessing the past and merely acknowledging those things already provided for us. Thus, since our request has already been granted when we pray in line with the Word of God, we can thank Him for the answer at the time we pray, and say to Him, "I believe that I receive it now, in Jesus' Name!" Faulty future faith, on the other hand, always interjects some period of time subsequent to the present rather than dealing with an immediate answer. Based on the verse quoted above, everything we might ask God to do for us is already done, and offered to each of us as a gift. Therefore, an important focus for Christians is to learn to receive from the Lord, and avoid faulty future faith.

# Questions for Study and Discussion from Chapter 3

1. Explain why man is considered a "speaking spirit."
2. Why can faith be thought of as "standing in the gap?"
3. How does faulty future faith contradict the Word of God?
4. How are the words, "I'll believe it when I see it" based in fear?
5. Explain the past tense of believing the promises of God.

# Prayer Concerning Faulty Future Faith

Father, I come in Jesus' Name to confess my struggle with faulty future faith. I thank you that I can now discern where I have been missing it in believing Your Word and praying in faith. Please forgive me for my prior unbelief. I ask You now to help me with both believing and praying in line with Your Word. Thank You for opening my understanding to walking by faith and not by sight. Lord, whether I feel it or not, whether I see it or not, I believe I receive this answer to my prayer. In Jesus' Name I pray, Amen.

# CHAPTER 4

**OFFENCE**

One characteristic of people in general is that most will commonly take offence at many different things. An individual who has become offended may exhibit any one or combinations of emotions such as anger, resentment, indignation, ruffled pride, hurt feelings, dissatisfaction, or displeasure. Some situations in life, for instance, may appear to favor one person while slighting another. While nothing was directly performed against this latter individual, the result is perceived inequity and therefore justification for offence. This may or may not grow into behaviors of anger and resentment, but the point to be made is that a seemingly harmless set of circumstances resulted in one or more persons having become offended.

A scriptural example of offence is as follows:

23 But he turned, and said unto Peter, Get thee behind me, Satan: thou art an offence unto me: for thou savourest not the things that be of God, but those that be of men. (Matt. 16:23, KJV)

Some writers have described the situation in this verse as an example of the law of double reference, such that a statement is directed to one person and simultaneously to an invisible second entity. In this instance, Jesus was addressing both Peter and Satan at the same time. The primary rebuke was centered squarely on Satan, but Peter had unwittingly allowed himself to be used as a puppet or tool of the devil to deal with Jesus. The Lord had just told the disciples that He would have to go to Jerusalem and suffer at the hands of the Jewish religious leaders and ultimately be crucified, (Matt. 16:21-22). However, impetuous Peter spoke up and attempted to correct Jesus by saying that such a fate would not befall the Lord. However well meaning the words of Peter may have been, he was speaking against what Jesus knew awaited Him and God's will for ultimately fulfilling His purpose on Earth.

A critical point to be brought out of Matthew 16:23 is that Jesus called Satan "an offence." The word translated "offence" is also translated as "hindrance," "stumbling block," "obstacle," "trap," or "scandal" in other versions of the Bible. Perhaps most interesting of these definitions of offence is that of being a "trap" or "scandal." The word in the Greek (*skandalizo*) refers to an offence, but the Greek word (*skandalon*) associated with offence refers to a trap. Specifically, animal trappers commonly apply or impale bait on a stick within a trapping mechanism. When an animal attempts to eat the bait offered on the bait stick, the energy stored in the trap, snare or deadfall is released, and the beast is caught and/or killed. In other words, offence is <u>bait for a trap</u> that Satan uses against us, and we fall victim to his nefarious efforts when we take that bait. When we refuse to become offended, we avoid the trap.

So what is the basis for offence? Some psychologists believe that our personal expectations of situations and/or interactions with others can often be contradicted, ignored, belittled, or openly attacked by individuals for an entire range of reasons. The end result of such negative impacts on our expectations is offence. The current culture of social media appears to have added immensely to the sheer amount of offence being encountered or maliciously dished out at every conceivable opportunity. If one takes the position that human beings are pretty much the same today as they were in ages gone by, then a paradigm shift has occurred in how we process perceived negative input or constructive criticism. Perhaps the stress from sensory overload, financial burdens, political instability, inculcated fears from repeated iterations of the same from the media, and so on could all be at the root source of so much offence taken in contemporary society. In a word, the decreasingly successful efficiency by each member of our culture has, despite a huge amount of individual efforts, produced a gradually declining rate of the ability to cope with circumstances, thus leading to offence.

As more and more individuals respond to offence by furthering the hurt and spreading it into their circles of influence, a downward spiral of malicious behaviors appears to grow. It matters not at all that the recipients of one persons' ire were not at fault or even involved with the original situation. The recipient simply did not deserve the wrath of the offended person, but got it anyway. Ideally, men and women should "switch off" the behaviors associated with being offended and simply not propagate it into any subsequent situation. Unfortunately, the "get even with the world" mentality of many persons prevents this.

We were told that offence would become a problem in these last of the last days. We can read the words:

1 This know also, that in the last days perilous times shall come.

2 For men shall be lovers of their own selves, covetous, boasters, proud, blasphemers, disobedient to parents, unthankful, unholy,

3 Without natural affection, trucebreakers, false accusers, incontinent, fierce, despisers of those that are good,

4 Traitors, heady, highminded, lovers of pleasures more than lovers of God;

5 Having a form of godliness, but denying the power thereof: from such turn away. (2 Tim. 3:1-7, KJV)

The disintegration of, and sharp divisions within, society today are unlike anything seen in our lifetimes. True, there have always been factions and splinter groups, but the United States, for instance, has seen a rise in racial strife that often dominates the headlines. The inexplicable aspect of the societal divisions is that these have crept into, and remained strong in, the church. One writer went so far as to state that Sunday church services reveal the most racial societal division of any day of the week. Far from accommodating diversity, many congregations are sharply racially delineated. One fabricated story was circulated that when a man of color attempted to worship in a church in which he would have been a singular minority, the ushers firmly escorted him out on to the steps at the front of the building. This gentleman sat there on those steps weeping with his head down, and then suddenly noticed a pair of sandal-clad feet appear in front of him. Looking up into the face of the individual standing there, the fellow recognized that it was Jesus Himself. When the Lord inquired as to why the man was sitting on the church steps crying, He was told, "All I wanted to do was worship God with these folks! That's all I wanted to do, but they wouldn't let me in!" Jesus then nodded understandingly and said, "Don't feel too badly about that... I've been trying to get in there Myself for years, and they won't let Me in either!"

A key point to be made about the Word of God is that Satan exerts great effort in order to nullify its effects in the lives of people, up to and including bringing offence. We can read this in Matthew 13:18-21.

18 Hear ye therefore the parable of the sower.

19 When any one heareth the word of the kingdom, and understandeth it not, then cometh the wicked one, and catcheth away that which was sown in his heart. This is he which received seed by the way side.

20 But he that received the seed into stony places, the same is he that heareth the word, and anon with joy receiveth it;

21 Yet hath he not root in himself, but dureth for a while: for when tribulation or persecution ariseth because of the word, by and by he is offended. (KJV)

The offence indicated in verse 21 above came because of apparently unexpected persecution and/or tribulation in the life of the hearer. Here is a very clear case of the *scandalon,* the baited stick of a trap, set by Satan disguised as tribulation or persecution. The person took the bait, and the trap was sprung. The result was that offence was created within this individual. This man could have refused the bait, and just went on with his life, but there was a problem: shallowness of the spiritual soil in the heart for the seed of the Word of God. With no significant depth of penetration into the spiritual soil of his heart, his shallowness ("no root in himself") did not permit sustained refusal for the bait of the trap. A natural seed may appear to flourish in a location with no significant depth of soil. However, when the sun beats down on the shallow ground, it becomes dry, hard, and unable to sustain the plant. The Word of God suffers the same fate in situations of offence in shallow individuals.

It is noteworthy that offence can actually be seen in the context of something quite positive. An example of this is:

30 What shall we say then? That the Gentiles, which followed not after righteousness, have attained to righteousness, even the righteousness which is of faith.

31 But Israel, which followed after the law of righteousness, hath not attained to the law of righteousness.

32 Wherefore? Because they sought it not by faith, but as it were by the works of the law. For they stumbled at that stumbling stone;

33 As it is written, Behold, I lay in Sion a stumblingstone
and rock of offence: and whosoever believeth on him shall
not be ashamed. (Rom. 9:30-33, KJV)

Jesus is referred to as the cornerstone of the church (Eph. 2:20),
and as such became the rock that upset the apple cart of the Jews who
sought righteousness by works under the Mosaic Law. These Hebrew
leaders and teachers were most likely sincere in their efforts, they were
just sincerely wrong. The law of righteousness by faith presented a
paradigm shift in religious thinking such that they had to believe on
and receive Jesus as their messiah. Unfortunately, this was too great
a leap (a "leap of faith") for them to endure, and the Rock of God
became an offence, not because of intended harm but rather because
of divine Love. In contemporary terms, we might characterize this rock
of offence as personifying "tough love." It was not at all the will of
God for these sincere Jewish leaders to fall away and miss the gift
of righteousness. Indeed, one might go so far as to state that the
inculcated Mosaic Law was actually the trap, the *scandalon*, which
caused their efforts to have come to naught.

So what is to be said about offence for the contemporary
Christian? Perhaps the most significant point to be made is: "Giving
no offence in any thing, that the ministry be not blamed" (2 Cor.
6:3, KJV). We are ambassadors for Christ (2 Cor. 5:20), and as such
represent the Lord in our words and deeds. For there to be deserved
reproach heaped upon any such ambassador is an open door for offence
in unbelievers. We have been commissioned as the light of the world
(Matt. 5:14), and must not have the divine light of the Lord shrouded
by inappropriate conversation, behaviors (or lack thereof), etc. It is a
fact that some persons in society will find fault even with both the pure
truth of the Word of God and consistently chaste behavior in the lives
of believers. Such eventualities boil down to a decision of offending
God or offending man. We cannot control the thoughts and reactions

of other people, so they will stand or fall on their own. A Christian, on the other hand, should seek to honor the Lord regardless of how others perceive his or her actions.

We are called to be faithful to the Word of God. Likewise, we are all to be faithful ministers of the Word of God! We cannot let our divine light shine if we remain "Closet Christians" and expect others to be impacted by our lives. Learning to avoid offence, having patience in those situations and circumstances that would otherwise cause a worldly "carnal" natural man to take issue, is a part of our walk of faith. Indeed, we are told: " Woe unto the world because of offences! for it must needs be that offences come; but woe to that man by whom the offence cometh!" (Matt. 18:7, KJV). We are to expect opportunities to take offence in this life, but we must not be the cause of those offences in the lives of others. As we are on our guard against offence, we defeat Satan so that he will not "...get an advantage of us: for we are not ignorant of his devices" (2 Cor. 2:11, KJV).

All of us make mistakes, and so learning to avoid offence is a process during which our going on to perfection in Christ will see some slips in this regard. Let each reader of these words resolve to begin anew the effort to daily be wary of the *scandalon* of the traps Satan sets for us. Refuse to take the bait leading to offence presented by whatever circumstances we encounter. As we operate more and more in the agape' love of God, we will be increasingly sincere and without offence till the coming of our Lord Jesus Christ (Phil. 1:10).

# Questions for Discussion

1) How is the "tough love" of the Lord related to the Jewish Sanhedrin and the Mosaic Law?

2) Explain how offence is related to the parable of the sower.

3) What is the relationship between baited traps and the phenomenon of offence in people?

4) How can what appear to be harmless situations result in offence manifesting in individuals?

5) What kinds of modern day situations could possibly cause increased levels of offence?

# Prayer Concerning Offence

Father, I come in Jesus' Name to confess that I have allowed offence to come into my life. I can see now that each situation was a baited trap for me. Help me, Lord, to seek to honor You in spite of the comments and actions of others. Open my spiritual eyes, Jesus, to perceive the devices of Satan and his attempts to put me off the path of agape' love that You would have me to walk. I need Your strength and peace to saturate my mind such that I can truly be the ambassador for Jesus that You would have me to be. Thank You for enabling me to be a source of Your Light and Love to those around me. In Jesus' Name I pray. Amen.

# CHAPTER 5
# FEAR

Many persons believe that fear is merely a normal human emotion that can be either mitigated by learned behavior or go unchecked up to and including completely controlling a person as if he/she were paralyzed. A realization of impending potential unpleasantness or physical damage and pain is the most likely cause for such emotions. In some situations, an individual experiencing fear may attempt to conceal its presence by an outburst of anger directed at persons and/or objects in their immediate vicinity. In long-term anger exposure caused by circumstances outside of an individual's control, chronically repressing this anger results in various degrees of mental depression. Medical professionals also describe our internal reactions to the presence of fear as the "fight or flight" response. In this regard, when confronted with fear, a rapid evaluation of the situation by the person experiencing fear creates an assessment to either "run for your life!" or a fighting attitude of "you want a piece of me?" Clearly, the mere presence of fear in the life of an individual can affect their behavior, often in a negative context.

In stark contrast to the above, the Bible records many references to the "fear of the Lord." This sort of statement highlights a reverential acknowledgement of Who God is and that He is worthy of our highest esteem and respect. As such, then, individuals tailor their dealings with Jehovah on a level unmatched by anything else. People may also have a respectful fear for things such as machines and power tools. The import here is the understanding that improper utilization of said devices will result in serious bodily harm or death. As such, then, when used carefully and properly, everyday handling of such devices is perfectly safe.

The Bible also records, " For God hath not given us the spirit of fear; but of power, and of love, and of a sound mind" (2 Tim. 1:7, KJV). Quite apart from high regard or respect, this verse identifies fear as a spirit sent against us. Since God is not the author of this nefarious agent, the origin of it must be Satan. The sheer realization of this origin of fear can bring about very significant change in the lives of Christians. A discussion of this last point will serve as the basis for the remainder of this chapter.

God cannot be the author of the spirit of fear, since He is Love (1 John 4:8), and we are told, "There is no fear in love; but perfect love casteth out fear: because fear hath torment. He that feareth is not made perfect in love" (1 John 4:18, KJV). The stated result of harboring fear in oneself is "punishment" or literally "torment." We have gone so far as to incorporate the original Greek word *phobos* ("phobia") into our everyday vocabulary. A search on the internet will reveal a huge list of these phobias that apply to a mind-boggling array of fears. So, for instance, there is chronophobia or a fear of the passage of time as in impending death or imagined catastrophe. Indeed, there is even a detailed study of a condition called "prison neurosis" by incarcerated individuals brought on by their surroundings. Some persons suffer from nyctophobia, or a fear of the dark. This may be common in young children, but when older individuals including adults harbor such fear, it is definitely a problem. A widespread series of phobias concerns various animals causing fear. One of these is arachnophobia, or the fear of spiders. Another is entomophobia or the fear of insects in general. Other common phobias include acrophobia, the fear of heights, and claustrophobia, the fear of being in a confined space. The list goes on and on, but for anyone subject to one or more of these, the fear and associated bodily ill effects are very real, and often debilitating.

Other reasons why God cannot be the source of tormenting fear are the well-documented effects of chronic fear. So, for instance, the large amounts of stomach acid produced during prolonged fear have been known to cause stomach ulcers. Appetite suppression and/or the inability to keep consumed food down without subsequent emesis during protracted tormenting fear tends to produce both muscle and general body wasting. An obvious outward symptom of such long-term fear is "sunken in eyes" wherein the protective fat pads behind the eyeballs have been depleted in the individual. Hypertension and other cardiovascular problems are also very common in persons suffering from long-term fear. The list goes on and on concerning the deleterious effects of prolonged fear. The Bible records, "Beloved, I wish above all things that thou mayest prosper and be in health, even as thy soul prospereth" (3 John 2, KJV). Since it is God's stated desire that we be in health, the preceding abnormal conditions (and many others) cannot be from the Lord or else He would be contradicting Himself.

A keynote symptom concerning the presence of fear is that of "worry." Indeed, some persons could be considered champion worriers, in that they envision a life without incessant worry as abnormal, i.e., constant worry is to them very "normal." Many of these individuals have learned this sort of emotional distress from their immediate family and previous generations. If one member of such a clan shuns the otherwise ubiquitous preoccupation with worry, they are often considered to be hard-hearted, irresponsible, and uncaring by the family. This sort of thinking is in direct contradiction to the Bible, which admonishes us:

25 "Therefore I tell you, do not be anxious about your life, what you shall eat or what you shall drink, nor about your body, what you shall put on. Is not life more than food, and the body more than clothing?

26 Look at the birds of the air: they neither sow nor reap nor gather into barns, and yet your heavenly Father feeds them. Are you not of more value than they?

27 And which of you by being anxious can add one cubit to his span of life?

28 And why are you anxious about clothing? Consider the lilies of the field, how they grow; they neither toil nor spin;

29 yet I tell you, even Solomon in all his glory was not arrayed like one of these.

30 But if God so clothes the grass of the field, which today is alive and tomorrow is thrown into the oven, will he not much more clothe you, O men of little faith?

31 Therefore do

not be anxious, saying, 'What shall we eat?' or 'What shall we drink?' or 'What shall we wear?'

32 For the Gentiles seek all these things; and your heavenly Father knows that you need them all.

33 But seek first his kingdom and his righteousness, and all these things shall be yours as well.

34 "Therefore do not be anxious about tomorrow, for tomorrow will be anxious for itself. Let the day's own trouble be sufficient for the day. (Matt. 6:25-34, RSV)

So what are these "champion worriers" and fear-laden persons to do in order to be free from the walls of mental incarceration they have endured for many days? First and foremost, such individuals must understand the origin of their fear. As stated previously, fear is a spirit sent against us from the kingdom of darkness ruled by Satan. They must recognize they are literally under attack by an invisible enemy agent. The Bible records, "My people are destroyed for lack of knowledge" (Hos. 4:6, KJV). Thus so long as Christians believe that "fear" is merely an emotional condition they possess, they will never adequately fight back against it. When the truth is known about their situation, persons targeted by this satanic entity can begin to scripturally oppose it.

The next thing such persons must learn is what the Bible has to say about resisting and defeating these nefarious beings. A starting point is "And they overcame him by the blood of the Lamb, and by the word of their testimony..." (Rev. 12:11, KJV). The "him" in that verse is Satan, the "Lamb" is Jesus, and the things we speak constitute our testimony. The struggle we face is in our mind, and we must understand that fear often creates a cerebral fortress or "stronghold" defying natural means to dislodge it. The Bible states:

> 3 For though we live in the world, we do not wage war as the world does.
>
> 4 The weapons we fight with are not the weapons of the world. On the contrary, they have divine power to demolish strongholds.
>
> 5 We demolish arguments and every pretension that sets itself up against the knowledge of God, and we take captive every thought to make it obedient to Christ. (2 Cor. 10:3-5, NIV)

So if the weapons with which we are to fight are spiritual in nature rather than the traditional guns, bombs, and bullets of natural warfare, what are they and how do we employ them to resist the spirit of fear? First and foremost in this regard can be found in Philippians 2:9-11

9 Wherefore God also hath highly exalted him, and given him a name which is above every name:

10 That at the name of Jesus every knee should bow, of things in heaven, and things in earth, and things under the earth;

11 And that every tongue should confess that Jesus Christ is Lord, to the glory of God the Father. (KJV)

Initially, then, we are to use the Name of Jesus to confront the spirit of fear. Why? The spirit of fear is merely a "thing with a name," and as such is subject to the spiritual power contained in Jesus' Name. Although a discussion of the details is far beyond the scope of this book, it is noteworthy to interject the fact that in the realm of the spirit, names are of supreme importance. In the passage quoted from Philippians, the very highest name in the universe is that of Jesus. Military personnel are acutely aware that regardless of the person wearing the uniform displaying a higher rank, there must be respect to, and obedience to commands from that individual. These actions are mandatory. Just so, spiritual forces likewise recognize the authority of names, and in this instance, the very highest Name is Jesus.

Another weapon to be used against the spirit of fear is found in Matthew 18:18. " Verily I say unto you, Whatsoever ye shall bind on earth shall be bound in heaven: and whatsoever ye shall loose on earth shall be loosed in heaven" (KJV). The value of binding the spirit of fear is implied in the words, "Or else how can one enter into a strong man's house, and spoil his goods, except he first bind the strong man? and then he will spoil his house" (Matt. 12:29, KJV). The "strong man's house" referred to here is the stronghold (of fear, in this case) mentioned in Second Corinthians 10:4 quoted previously. Then when the spirit of fear is rendered helpless, it can be kicked out of the mind of the individual because it is written, "If the Son therefore shall make you free, ye shall be free indeed" (John 8:36, KJV).

So now to combine all of this information about dealing with the spirit of fear, the person under attack should first speak against that agent of darkness as follows: "In the Name of Jesus, I come against this spirit of fear. I plead the blood of Jesus against you, and bind you according to the Word of God. I exalt the Name of Jesus over you and command you to bow your knee to that Name. I demolish that stronghold you had set up in my mind, and my testimony is that I have been set free from you. The blood of Jesus and the Word of God have overcome you. Now get out and stay out, in Jesus' Name!"

Merely refuse to allow that thought pattern to reestablish itself in one's mind, and trust in the Lord that the spiritual weapons employed against that spirit of fear have done their job. Some individuals who have set themselves free in this manner report that the anxiety level and nervousness they previously were experiencing internally have been eliminated. "It is nothing like what it was before!" they say. We are not to live carelessly and ignore safety rules, but when unjustifiable fear of some situation or event tries again to rear its ugly head against us, we can decapitate that nefarious agent of darkness swiftly and effectively. By using the spiritual weapons described in this chapter, we can realize the truth of the statement, "He whom the Son sets free is free indeed!"

# Questions for Discussion

1) Why is it inaccurate to view fear as merely a human emotion to which all persons are subject?

2) Of what value is the Name of Jesus in dealing with fear?

3) Why is fear not as easy as "thinking about something else" to rid it from our minds?

4) What are some of the manifestations of fear in the lives of people?

5) What scriptures state that we are commanded not to worry?

# Prayer for Dealing With Fear

In the Name of Jesus, I come against this spirit of fear. I plead the blood of Jesus against you, and bind you according to the Word of God. I exalt the Name of Jesus over you and command you to bow your knee to that Name. I demolish that stronghold you had set up in my mind, and my testimony is that I have been set free from you. The blood of Jesus and the Word of God have overcome you. Now get out and stay out, in Jesus' Name!

# CHAPTER 6
# INTELLECTUALISM

Much of the contemporary church has succumbed to a spirit of intellectualism. This is not too unlike the situation in Biblical times wherein the leaders of the temple constituted a theocracy composed of Pharisees, Sadducees, and the Priests. Persons outside of this select clique were considered inferior, cursed, and unsuccessful in living under the Mosaic Law. In modern times, the university degrees and spiritual titles earned by, or given to, leadership constitute the basis for acknowledged respect and authority. While there is categorically nothing at all wrong with pursuing education and advancing in academic degrees, a line has been crossed and bridges burned when such intellectualism replaces the gospel in the lives of Christians.

The apostle Paul stated:

4 And my speech and my preaching was not with enticing words of man's wisdom, but in demonstration of the Spirit and of power:

5 That your faith should not stand in the wisdom of men, but in the power of God.

6 Howbeit we speak wisdom among them that are perfect: yet not the wisdom of this world, nor of the princes of this world, that come to nought:

7 But we speak the wisdom of God in a mystery, even the hidden wisdom, which God ordained before the world unto our glory:

> 8 Which none of the princes of this world knew: for had they known it, they would not have crucified the Lord of glory. (1 Cor. 2:4-8, KJV)

The Bible records that Paul was an extremely learned man and a standout among his peers. His stated concern in the passage quoted above, however, was that the wisdom of men was not sufficient to form the basis of faith in God. What is still worse, the emphasis on high tech in churches today has further removed the demonstration of the Spirit and power from many congregations. It is herein stated that there is nothing inherently wrong with high tech, and that it has been a blessing to many around the world by enabling the Word of God to reach multitudes of the unsaved. On the other hand, when the glory cloud that filled the Old Testament temple and/or the aromas from the altar of incense have been cheapened to include smoke machines to simulate the same, electronically controlled light shows and ear-piercingly loud music employed to capture and hold the attention of congregates, we have obviously crossed a dangerous line. Jesus and His disciples performed their ministry just fine having wonderful success without modern high tech!

It has become politically incorrect to preach on topics such as "sin" and "the blood of Jesus" in many religious circles today. We have apparently become so sophisticated in our "playing church" that such discussions are either beneath our dignity to deal with and/or are too messy to appeal to those in the padded pews. While our intellectualism has increased, the "demonstration of the Spirit and power" has coincidentally decreased to the point that expectation for a move of God seems to have been virtually extinguished. Indeed, a common statement heard today when prayer for God to act in the behalf of some situation in a person's life is, "Well, has it come to that?" Rather than seeking the Lord first in a critical need for some individual, the thought of Jesus intervening in the midst of what is going on is very lightly regarded.

So let us examine this oddity of intellectualism from a scriptural standpoint. In the book of Romans can be found the following passage.

21 Because that, when they knew God, they glorified him not as God, neither were thankful; but became vain in their imaginations, and their foolish heart was darkened.

22 Professing themselves to be wise, they became fools,

23 And changed the glory of the uncorruptible God into an image made like to corruptible man, and to birds, and fourfooted beasts, and creeping things. ((Rom. 1: 21-23, KJV)

28 And even as they did not like to retain God in their knowledge, God gave them over to a reprobate mind, to do those things which are not convenient;

29 Being filled with all unrighteousness, fornication, wickedness, covetousness, maliciousness; full of envy, murder, debate, deceit, malignity; whisperers,

30 Backbiters, haters of God, despiteful, proud, boasters, inventors of evil things, disobedient to parents,

31 Without understanding, covenantbreakers, without natural affection, implacable, unmerciful:

32 Who knowing the judgment of God, that they which commit such things are worthy of death, not only do the same, but have pleasure in them that do them. (Rom. 1: 28-32, KJV)

The apostle Paul was a Pharisee (Acts 26:5), and was known for his advanced knowledge of the Mosaic Law (Gal.1: 14, Acts 22: 3). His zeal for righteousness through the law, however, was swept away by the revelation of righteousness by grace through faith in Jesus. Indeed, he considered all of his learning and position among the Pharisees as "dung" after his salvation experience (Phil. 3: 8). Enter now this Jewish scholar criticizing highly educated Hebrew leaders and other generations of academia in stating that they were no longer wise, but had become fools! His basis for this contentious evaluation was that God had not been retained in their thinking, and had even been held to contempt by replacing the Lord with natural images and no longer worshiping Him. When it became clear that God had been pushed out of their thinking, they were given over to a reprobate mind. Their heart became darkened to the light of the Lord, and the laundry list of godless behaviors resulting from the same is still true in the lives of such persons today!

There are many fine institutions of higher learning today in which the Lord is both respected and His Word represented faithfully. However, there are many campuses, including seminaries, at which Biblical truths are openly mocked, class lectures presented denying such basic beliefs as the virgin birth of Jesus, His resurrection from the dead, and even that He is the Son of God. Graduates from such centers of humanistic culture then proceed out into the world to spread their reprobate mind and training to all that will listen. The danger of such intellectualism is, of course, that because of titles, college degrees, and ostensibly sophisticated conceptualization of Biblical refutations, many church goers have been led astray by believing that their leaders are "right."

Persons who deny that the spirit of intellectualism impacts contemporary congregations of church leaders need to be informed. Many has been the man of God who has dared to present the truths of the Bible, but which went contrary to his particular denominational training. When this sort of thing did not sit well with various people under his leadership, letters to the authorities of said denominations led to investigations of that pastor. When the accusations were substantiated, these preachers were given the left foot of fellowship and removed from their posts, never again being allowed to fill a pastorate in a church of that particular denomination. So in other words, so long as lies grounded in intellectual training were preached, everything was fine. However, when Biblical truth was shown as contrary to denominational thought, church splits, controversy and conflict, and ultimately firing of the minister occurred. Those who would deny that such occurs simply do not have the facts.

The spirit of intellectualism does not stop at the church organization level, however. It attacks families as well, and seeks to upset relationships within the same to the extent that in many cases one part of the family attends one church, and the others go elsewhere. God is not the author of confusion (1 Cor. 14: 33)! Nevertheless, an example of how this can occur even in close-knit families is instructive. For example, one young man confronted his parents about obvious contradictions being presented in church sermons: one thing was read from the Bible, other contradictory statements were presented in sermons, and yet another set of values were observed out in society. None of the three were in agreement, and the position taken by the fellow just mentioned was to tell his parents that they would be going to church by themselves unless something were done to make sense of it all. Ultimately, the family began "church hopping" to seek out a congregation blessed with leadership that did not perpetuate the confusion just described. Reportedly to their horror, this family could find no church home in their city that believed and preached the Bible, not condoning the humanism of the society around them. In a single stroke, the family split in terms of worshipping together at only one church. Indeed, when one of the pastors was caught in a plain-faced lie during one of his intellectual lectures (read "sermons"), reportedly a ministerial visit to the home of the parents was necessitated to attempt to assuage the situation. Unfortunately, such an attempted apology for intellectualism during a sermon was reportedly profoundly unsuccessful.

How is it, then, that highly educated persons could fall victim to a spirit of intellectualism? An answer can be found in the following passage of scripture.

> 12 Now we have received, not the spirit of the world, but the spirit which is of God; that we might know the things that are freely given to us of God.
>
> 13 Which things also we speak, not in the words which man's wisdom teacheth, but which the Holy Ghost teacheth; comparing spiritual things with spiritual.
>
> 14 But the natural man receiveth not the things of the Spirit of God: for they are foolishness unto him: neither can he know them, because they are spiritually discerned. (1 Cor. 2: 12-14, KJV)

The "natural man" denoted in verse fourteen above refers to someone that is not born again. This deficiency of the Spirit of God in their lives prevents them from being able to receive Biblical truths in their entirety. Yes, a basic understanding of words contained in a given scripture may be read and comprehended based on book knowledge. However, Biblical truths are spiritually discerned, and without the Holy Spirit dwelling in the spirit man of a person, scriptural teachings appear to be merely foolishness. Jesus Himself stated that you "must be born again." An example of this dichotomy in understanding can be seen in the following passage.

1 Here was a man of the Pharisees, named Nicodemus, a ruler of the Jews:

2 The same came to Jesus by night, and said unto him, Rabbi, we know that thou art a teacher come from God: for no man can do these miracles that thou doest, except God be with him.

3 Jesus answered and said unto him, Verily, verily, I say unto thee, Except a man be born again, he cannot see the kingdom of God.

4 Nicodemus saith unto him, How can a man be born when he is old? can he enter the second time into his mother's womb, and be born?

5 Jesus answered, Verily, verily, I say unto thee, Except a man be born of water and of the Spirit, he cannot enter into the kingdom of God.}

6 That which is born of the flesh is flesh; and that which is born of the Spirit is spirit.

7 Marvel not that I said unto thee, Ye must be born again.

8 The wind bloweth where it listeth, and thou hearest the sound thereof, but canst not tell whence it cometh, and whither it goeth: so is every one that is born of the Spirit.

9 Nicodemus answered and said unto him, How can these things be? (John 3: 1-9, KJV)

Nicodemus was reportedly a Pharisee and a member of the Sanhedrin. A highly educated man, this fellow recognized that the power of God was manifested through Jesus, but was dumbfounded by the concept of being "born again." His intellect would not allow the thought of birth to mean anything except passage through the womb of a woman. Here was the clearest delineation of the natural mind versus the mind of the Spirit. Nicodemus had a mindset anchored firmly in the natural world. However, Jesus was referring to the spirit of a man that was separated from God until that individual believed, received, and confessed Jesus into their "heart." Unlike the Sadducees, the Pharisees believed in the resurrection, but their belief was steeped in the legalism of the Mosaic Law, also known as intellectualism. When Jesus presented a paradigm shift that had occurred in the realm of the Spirit, Nicodemus was tied down to said Mosaic Law, and could not make the transition to spiritually entering the kingdom of God.

The failure realized by the apostle Paul after his preaching at Athens (see Acts chapter 17) was that merely using brainpower as an approach to reach the hearts of men was not enough! He resolved that from that point forward his emphasis would be on the demonstration of power of God following the Word that he preached. Just as in the days of Paul, a supernatural ministry with signs and wonders is what the world is hungry to receive. So when contemporary Christians share the Word of God with other be it from the pulpit, a Bible study group, or one-on-one ministry, we need to realize that the power of the Holy Spirit is available to confirm that Word. We need to press beyond timidity and step out in faith for God to bring manifestations of His power into the lives of those to whom we minister!

# Questions for Discussion

1) What was the approach of the apostle Paul to his listeners when he preached at Athens?

2) Athens was a very religious city with many temples and pagan religions, so why was Paul ineffective?

3) Why is intellectualism so honored, yet so lacking in indisputably authenticating the Word of God?

4) How likely will persons witnessing a supernatural ministry realize that God is speaking directly to them?

5) Explain the relevance of Mark chapter 16: 15-20 to defeating the spirit of intellectualism.

6) What message does Mark 16:17-18 hold for the contemporary Christian?

# Prayer for Dealing With Intellectualism

Heavenly Father, I come in Jesus' Name to ask Your forgiveness for substituting sophisticated-sounding church-speak for the clear teachings in Your Word. I likewise ask Your forgiveness for having allowed my expectations for manifestations of Holy Ghost power to have been replaced by satisfaction with the status quo. Lord, I ask you to help me renew my mind with the Word of God and begin rejecting contradictory teaching. God, I need Your help! I want to walk in the leading of the Holy Spirit and not lean on intellectualism for my spiritual direction. I believe and receive by faith new demonstrations of power and love in my life through focusing on You and Your Word, and not the "enticing words of man's wisdom." I give You all the praise and the glory for this, in Jesus' Name. Amen.

# CHAPTER 7
# DISCONTENTMENT

In the gospel of John chapter four, verses five through twenty-nine, an event is recorded wherein Jesus met a Samaritan woman at a well of water and spoke with her. While such a lengthy passage of scripture is too long to insert here, a selection will suffice to bring out the main import for this discussion.

13 Jesus answered and said unto her, Whosoever drinketh of this water shall thirst again:

14 But whosoever drinketh of the water that I shall give him shall never thirst; but the water that I shall give him shall be in him a well of water springing up into everlasting life.

15 The woman saith unto him, Sir, give me this water, that I thirst not, neither come hither to draw.

16 Jesus saith unto her, Go, call thy husband, and come hither.

17 The woman answered and said, I have no husband. Jesus said unto her, Thou hast well said, I have no husband:

18 For thou hast had five husbands; and he whom thou now hast is not thy husband: in that saidst thou truly. (John 4:13-18, KJV)

In the natural, this discussion appears to be centered squarely on drinking some water. A closer inspection of the words brings out the fact that Jesus was referring to something very much greater than mere liquid water. The alleviation of thirst was, of course, the original purpose the Samaritan woman had in mind. The prospect of somehow being given water internally such that frequent visits to Jacob's well and the laborious process of carrying of water home would no longer be necessary was obviously intriguing to this resident of Sycar. However, when Jesus instructed her to go bring her husband so the two of them could speak with Him, "thirst" of another nature was revealed in this Samaritan woman. She had previously had five husbands (v.18), and was now in a living arrangement with yet another man. Although Jesus was not recorded as using the specific term in dealing with this individual, He was pointing out that she was not "satisfied" in life. She was not content with any of the five husbands, was now living with a sixth fellow, and her coming to the well to draw water at an hour far later than the usual morning times further revealed that she was trying to avoid contact with the other women from the town. In a word, she was suffering from discontentment.

A person harboring a spirit of discontentment can manifest a lifestyle that has characteristics quite different from a satisfied individual. So in this particular case, the woman went from partner to partner trying to suffice some perceived emotional need, but to no avail. The obvious mindset of this woman was that "he's no good" and this next one is "likewise no good," never entertaining the possibility that the problem centered on her, not the parade of men in her life. In contemporary society, there are people that jump from job to job and one occupation to another merely on a whim because of this same spirit of discontentment. There are individuals that attempt to assuage their inner struggle with discontentment by purchasing clothing. In this way, they justify repeated spending on multiple garments duplicating those in their closets, even though they already have many days' worth of sufficient shoes, jeans, tops, jackets, etc. Being "in style" has nothing to do with effectively calming their inner discontentment!

The spirit of discontentment can attack individuals based on their perceived need to conform to some image foisted on them by their environment, media advertising or whatever have you. So it can be observed that big persons are constantly trying to lose weight to be skinny, and that thin people are drinking all manner of protein and high calorie products trying to put on weight, etc. This is not to denigrate the efforts of many to better themselves and effect a healthier lifestyle and its benefits, however. Some other individuals purchase a brand new car only to soon return it to the dealership and trade it in on another different model because the first "wasn't just right." Before too long, they are back again to go further in debt getting yet another exchange for a still different vehicle because they found fault with the second car.

The spirit of discontentment driving these aforesaid individuals in their aberrant lifestyles creates an inner dissatisfaction void in any one or many areas. Incessantly remodeling and repainting an area of one's home is prima facie evidence of this. Staring at the same color walls for very long stirs up a tension within them that only new paint, new carpeting, new furniture, new window treatments, etc. will theoretically allow them to find rest, only to be repeated again in the near future. Financial indebtedness often accompanies the lifestyles of such persons, and they justify their plight by convincing themselves that "this is just normal for me."

The Bible teaches that we can come to a place such that we are not driven into debt or live constantly dissatisfied. We can find the words:

> 11 Not that I speak in respect of want: for I have learned, in whatsoever state I am, therewith to be content.

> 12 I know both how to be abased, and I know how to abound: every where and in all things I am instructed both to be full and to be hungry, both to abound and to suffer need. (Phil 4:11-12, KJV)

Whereas the process of learning can take many forms, the key teaching in the above passage of scripture is that of "whatsoever state." In this case, the "state" is merely a temporary condition subject to change. The obvious implication of verse eleven above was that the apostle Paul had encountered a number of situational changes in life. Some of these included imprisonment, attempted assassination, rejection by his peers, and so on, but there were life lessons he acquired through each as well as in the transition from one to the other. His endurance, however, was not in some stoicism or fatalistic numbness to his surroundings. Rather, he came through each with the knowledge that "I can do all things through Christ which strengtheneth me" (Phil. 4:13, KJV). By his relying on the Lord and the leading of the Holy Spirit, Paul had learned in all things to trust in God.

It seems that the apostle Paul had tapped into an amazing truth: "But godliness with contentment is great gain" (1 Timothy 6:6, KJV). The contentment referred to here is that of a mind freed from murmuring and complaining, apparently because such statements are a direct result of the spirit of discontentment. So many persons are plainly jealous of the promotions, acquisitions, accomplishments, and lifestyles of others saying, "That could have been (or should have been) me, rather than them." An interesting passage of scripture speaks to this mindset in Psalms 73.

3 For I was envious at the foolish, when I saw the prosperity of the wicked.

4 For there are no bands in their death: but their strength is firm.

5 They are not in trouble as other men; neither are they plagued like other men.

17 Until I went into the sanctuary of God; then understood I their end.

18 Surely thou didst set them in slippery places: thou castedst them down into destruction.

19 How are they brought into desolation, as in a moment! they are utterly consumed with terrors. (Ps. 73: 3-5 and 17-19, KJV)

Many has been the time that the media have reported about a movie star, famous political personality, sports hero, etc., the possessions of whom were more than heart could desire, only to end their own life through overdoses or tragic circumstances. Only after one of these persons has died has the truth been revealed to the public by close associates and friends of the now deceased personality's secretly miserable life of depression, anxiety attacks, physical health issues brought on by alcohol, tobacco, drugs and so on. Just as the scripture stated in Psalm 73: 19 quoted above that their lives were brought to and abrupt end in a moment! The problem, it would appear, was that money, possessions, fame and cultural envy were not sufficient to have produced contentment in their lives. Consequently, they were no better off emotionally, and likely spiritually as well, than were the average non-celebrity persons who sought after the Lord and His godliness in their lives.

The book of Ecclesiastes has much to say regarding a lifestyle of discontentment, particularly in chapter two of that part of the Bible. Solomon, the author of the book, details a litany of pleasures and voluptuous living that brought no contentment. He had the resources to have produced beautiful gardens, orchards of many types of trees, constructed houses and various great works, had very many male and female servants, and so on, yet referred to it all as "vanity." The word translated as "vanity" has been also variously translated as "worthless," "empty," "fruitless," "frustration," "nothingness" and so on. If the splendor in the life of this man Solomon could be encapsulated into the equivalent of an idol or idols to be sought after without contentment, what does his evaluation hold in meaning for contemporary Christians today? How much more could be said for the effectiveness of the spirit of discontentment sent against persons today concerning comparatively petty things?

The fact that the vastness of Solomon's riches, possessions, accomplishments and experiences brought him no contentment is prima facie evidence that the human spirit has the capacity for far more than this natural world has to offer. As if echoing these musings of Solomon, Shakespeare stated in Macbeth the famous lines:

Out, out, brief candle!
Life's but a walking shadow, a poor player
That struts and frets his hour upon the stage
And then is heard no more: it is a tale
Told by an idiot, full of sound and fury,
Signifying nothing." (Macbeth, Act 5, Scene 5)

Indeed, this is precisely why it is so necessary for each person to heed the words of Rev. 3: 20: "Behold, I stand at the door, and knock: if any man hear my voice, and open the door, I will come in to him, and will sup with him, and he with me" (KJV). Literally the Lord is stating here that He is the only thing that has the monumental stature to fill the human spirit! Anything less will merely lead to seeking after things and natural phenomena that will ultimately prove to be vanity, chasing after what amounts to an idol! We therefore defeat the spirit of discontentment by learning to trust in and lean on the Lord. Some experiences may not be enjoyable, some may bring heartache and tears, but when the cry of our heart is genuinely that of "Not my will, but thine be done" we can more fully comprehend the words:

23 From Jehovah [are] the steps of a man, They have been prepared, And his way he desireth.

24 When he falleth, he is not cast down, For Jehovah is sustaining his hand. (Ps 37: 23-24, YLT)

# Questions For Discussion

1) What is the relationship between discontentment and a complaining lifestyle?

2) How are financial insolvency and spiritual discontentment potentially interconnected?

3) In spite of his wisdom, did Solomon exhibit behaviors that resemble discontentment?

4) Why are the truths contained in Psalm 73 effective against the spirit of discontentment?

5) Jesus used the situation of natural thirst as a strategy for revealing what spiritual condition?

# Prayer for Dealing With Discontentment

Heavenly Father, I ask in Jesus' Name that You forgive me for my pride in assuming that my plans are superior to Your plans for me. Forgive me for entertaining the thoughts of that spirit of discontentment such that I have complained and murmured about my life situations. I ask You, Lord, for emotional and spiritual contentment to rule in my life instead of that former discontentment. Herein I seek after godliness and Your Will for my life rather than the worldly substitutes for the same that I have sought out in the past. Help me come to realize, Jesus, that I can do all things through you as the Holy

Spirit leads me. I ask these things and receive them by faith in Jesus' Name. Amen.

# CHAPTER 8
# DECEPTION

A major source of spiritual assaults against Christians comes from the spirit of deception. The aim of this agent of darkness is to cause individuals to receive as true that which is false or invalid so as to prevent them from comprehending the truth. Lying is a common form of deception, and the Bible declares that the devil is the father of lies:

> 8 Ye are of your father the devil, and the lusts of your father ye will do. He was a murderer from the beginning, and abode not in the truth, because there is no truth in him. When he speaketh a lie, he speaketh of his own: for he is a liar, and the father of it. (John 8:44, KJV)

The spirit of deception appears early in the Bible, as we can read in Gen. 3: 13, "Then the Lord God said to the woman, 'What is this you have done?' The woman said, 'The serpent deceived me, and I ate'" (NIV). Many sermons could be preached from this single verse, but the point for this discussion is that Eve commented the serpent "deceived" her, or in other words, caused her to err. Both Adam and Eve were already like gods, but the desire to be "made wise" overrode the admonition of the Lord not to eat of the forbidden fruit. The rest, as the saying goes, is history.

Some persons might suggest that such a nefarious agent as a spirit of deception was merely an Old Testament phenomenon. However, this is simply not the case. The Bible records, "For many deceivers are entered into the world, who confess not that Jesus Christ is come in the flesh. This is a deceiver and an antichrist" (2 John 7, KJV).

The fact that the Word of God plainly states the world has "many deceivers" is just as relevant for today as in Biblical days. Indeed, we are admonished to test the authenticity of anyone purporting to be a prophet of God:

> 1 Beloved, believe not every spirit, but try the spirits whether they are of God: because many false prophets are gone out into the world.

> 2 Hereby know ye the Spirit of God: Every spirit that confesseth that Jesus Christ is come in the flesh is of God:

> 3 And every spirit that confesseth not that Jesus Christ is come in the flesh is not of God: and this is that spirit of antichrist, whereof ye have heard that it should come; and even now already is it in the world. (1 John 4:1-3, KJV)

As pointed out in the passage from Second John verse seven above, the antichrist spirit is just another type of deceiver sent against Christians and the world in general. The standard against which all teaching about the Lord is the Word of God. Every mystic talking head does not necessarily represent God, and while every person is entitled to his or her opinion, cerebral creations from self-professed prophetic individuals that do not accurately reflect the Word of God are to be categorically rejected. The ultimate goal of any spirit of deception regarding the Word of God is to prevent individuals from perceiving the truth of the Bible, rejecting the same, and thus not receiving salvation in Jesus.

The spirit of deception does not always come against a person through the agency of another individual. Indeed, the Bible states that a man or woman can have "self-deception" from "The pride of your heart" (Obed. 1:3, RSV). We can find the words, " If any man among you seem to be religious, and bridleth not his tongue, but deceiveth his own heart, this man's religion is vain" (James 1:26, KJV). The import of this verse is considerable. First of all, this passage clearly states that an individual can deceive his or her own heart. This self-deception can take many forms and come from many directions, but the specific source of self-deception denoted here is that of a religious facade. Jesus addressed this sort of charade when He stated:

> 8 This people draweth nigh unto me with their mouth, and honoureth me with their lips; but their heart is far from me.

> 9 But in vain they do worship me, teaching for doctrines the commandments of men. (Matt. 15:8-9, KJV)

The problem with the "religious" indictment aspect of James 1:26 above is apparently the observation of rituals, seasons, and ceremonies without sanctity of the heart for the same. In other words, this amounts to much ado about merely going through the motions for the sake of appearances. Combined with the verses from Matthew 15: 8-9, an additional self-deception takes place when the teachings from such a religious-appearing person do not line up with the Word of God and instead are merely man-made holy sounding platitudes.

The second form of self-deception indicated in James 1: 26 comes from the phrase "bridleth not his tongue." In this regard, the individual may have mastered a degree of "church-speak" vocabulary and learned to verbalize the same at appropriate times. However, the diction of this person may be anything but sanctified outside of the boundaries of familiar ceremonies and rituals. Indeed, the Word records:

> 34 O generation of vipers, how can ye, being evil, speak good things? for out of the abundance of the heart the mouth speaketh.

> 35 A good man out of the good treasure of the heart bringeth forth good things: and an evil man out of the evil treasure bringeth forth evil things.

36 But I say unto you, That every idle word that men shall speak, they shall give account thereof in the day of judgment.

37 For by thy words thou shalt be justified, and by thy words thou shalt be condemned. (Matt. 12:34-37, KJV)

Why was this such a priority with Jesus? He addressed this form of self-deception concerning supposed piety of religious persons and people in general when He stated:

18 But those things which proceed out of the mouth come forth from the heart; and they defile the man.

19 For out of the heart proceed evil thoughts, murders, adulteries, fornications, thefts, false witness, blasphemies:

20 These are the things which defile a man: but to eat with unwashen hands defileth not a man. (Matt. 15:18-20, KJV)

The Jews were very strict on things like hand washing prior to eating. Even certain types of food that were eaten were considered a source of defilement. In this passage from Matthew 15: 18-20, Jesus indicates that spoken words are what genuinely defile an individual. Coupled with the passage from Matthew 12:34-35 cited above, the vocabulary utilized by a person literally displays what is in his or her heart in abundance. Thus, when someone appears to be religious, but their tongue is not controlled or disciplined to speaking the Word of God, then they have defiled themselves through self-deception in their heart and their religion is in vain. In other words, their guilt of sin comes not from behaviors but from the words they speak!

A still different sort of self-deception can be seen in the account of Samson in Judges chapter sixteen. To paraphrase the situation leading up to the relevant details of this man's life, Samson had married a woman not of the Hebrews, and this Delilah was a scheming individual. When she had finally provoked Samson to reveal the source of his great strength, which was his uncut hair of a Nazirite vow, she hired a barber to shave it off. As she had done three times in the past, Delilah woke Samson and declared that the Philistines had come to take him captive. In all of these previous occasions, Samson awoke and defeated all of the attempted restraints placed upon him. In this last instance, however, we can read:

> 19 And she made him sleep upon her knees; and she called for a man, and she caused him to shave off the seven locks of his head; and she began to afflict him, and his strength went from him.

> 20 And she said, The Philistines be upon thee, Samson. And he awoke out of his sleep, and said, I will go out as at other times before, and shake myself. And he wist not that the Lord was departed from him.

> 21 But the Philistines took him, and put out his eyes, and brought him down to Gaza, and bound him with fetters of brass; and he did grind in the prison house. (Judg. 16:19-21, KJV)

In this passage of scripture, verse twenty reveals that Samson was in the habit of getting up from sleep and shaking himself in such a way that his great strength returned and allowed him to go about with impunity. His shaven head had defiled his Nazirite vow, however, and he was taken captive. Literally, the self-deception of Samson lay squarely in his habituation. The matrimonial betrayal by his Philistine harlot wife was self-inflicted, and shaking as performed in the past was to no avail.

Perhaps the lesson to be learned from the account of Samson is that contemporary Christians may be going through the motions of rites and rituals, but when a crisis arises, whatever may have worked in the past as a respite from the same circumstances now is useless. Like Samson, we are virtual captives of our own habituation. Indeed, each of us may have entertained a spirit of self-deception for some time, not realizing that such a path was ultimately leading to some level of self-destruction. It is recorded in Proverbs 14:12, "There is a way which seemeth right unto a man, but the end thereof are the ways of death" (KJV). Jesus stated, "...I am the way, the truth, and the life: no man cometh unto the Father, but by me" (John 14:6, KJV). The self-deception of habitual religious patterns, rituals and ceremonies obviously must be replaced by getting our heart right with God and following the leading of the Holy Spirit in our lives.

Yet another form of self-deception can be found in these words from Romans 12:3, "For I say, through the grace given unto me, to every man that is among you, not to think of himself more highly than he ought to think" (KJV). Another way of stating "think of himself more highly than he ought to think" is to simply use the term "pride." Interestingly the Bible states," For all that is in the world, the lust of the flesh, and the lust of the eyes, and the pride of life, is not of the Father, but is of the world" (1 John 2:16, KJV). These three items encompass all worldly sin, so that the self-deception of thinking more highly of oneself than is proper easily falls into the last of these categories.

A common psychological ploy of many persons suffering from an inferiority complex is to belittle and berate others such that this individual believes he or she has now elevated their own status above those verbally put down. Unfortunately, people with a high level of pride often do the same thing, i.e., supposing that they are somehow more important, their efforts more valuable, their function of a higher nature, etc. than those around them. The conversation of this latter sort of person often makes them quite obnoxious!

A key point for Christians to remember is that the "church" is not an organization, but rather an organism that is the living Body of Christ.

> 12 For as the body is one, and hath many members, and all the members of that one body, being many, are one body: so also is Christ.

> 13 For by one Spirit are we all baptized into one body, whether we be Jews or Gentiles, whether we be bond or free; and have been all made to drink into one Spirit.

> 14 For the body is not one member, but many.

> 15 If the foot shall say, Because I am not the hand, I am not of the body; is it therefore not of the body?

> 16 And if the ear shall say, Because I am not the eye, I am not of the body; is it therefore not of the body?

> 17 If the whole body were an eye, where were the hearing? If the whole were hearing, where were the smelling?

> 18 But now hath God set the members every one of them in the body, as it hath pleased him.

> 19 And if they were all one member, where were the body?

> 20 But now are they many members, yet but one body. (1 Cor. 12:12-20, KJV)

The personal desire for recognition via thinking more highly than they ought to think in some individuals can be destructive for both the body of Christ as well as themselves. When the spirit of deception has been allowed to operate unchecked in a congregation, church splits and "backdoor revivals" (by persons leaving that church) often result.

So how can a person begin to deal with a spirit of self-deception? We can find a starting point in the passage of James 1:22-25.

22 But be ye doers of the word, and not hearers only, deceiving your own selves.

23 For if any be a hearer of the word, and not a doer, he is like unto a man beholding his natural face in a glass:

24 For he beholdeth himself, and goeth his way, and straightway forgetteth what manner of man he was.

25 But whoso looketh into the perfect law of liberty, and continueth therein, he being not a forgetful hearer, but a doer of the work, this man shall be blessed in his deed. (James 1:22-25, KJV)

There is something about doing the Word and not hearing it only that impacts the soul of an individual. Indeed, faith without works is dead (Jas. 2:26). As a parallel, some persons purport to be members of a particular church or denomination and will add, "...but I'm not practicing." If such an individual had not made that statement, there would be absolutely no indication of such membership in their life. In the same way some fellow seeking to justify his former athleticism might state, "I'm a football player." Truth be told this gentleman has not played a single down of football for at least ten years. His now pendulous abdomen would seriously hamper his successful completion of some team assignment on the playing field, let alone be likely prevent the uniform from fitting him in the first place!

Merely going to church however often and listening to a sermon, then leaving the building only to ignore what was presented for changes in one's lifestyle is dead faith. We must take the Word of God that we receive and allow it to begin affecting our thinking such that our behavior follows suite and begins to change. The spirit of self-deception is defeated as the continuing process of putting into practice the principles of the Bible chip away at former ungodliness. Thus as doers of the Word and not hearers only, we will encompass a godly lifestyle and begin to overcome former spiritual deceptions.

# Questions For Discussion

1) Why does the Bible admonish Christians to specifically interrogate spirits carried by certain persons?

2) Since people are creatures of habit, how is this dangerous for possible deception?

3) Having an opinion is one thing, but how are unscriptural teachings from leaders to be dealt with?

4) In what way can a person learn about the "heart" of another individual in a short time?

5) What is "vain worship" and how is it both dangerous and futile?

# Prayer For Dealing With Deception

Heavenly Father, I come in the Name of Jesus to thank you that according to your Word, you have given us a sound mind. I plead the blood of Jesus over my mind right now to shield me from the efforts of the spirit of deception. Lord, thank You for opening my spiritual eyes to clearly discern any attempts of deception sent against me. As I go through the remainder of this day, I thank You for continuing to bless me with Your protection from deceptive thoughts. Holy Spirit, I need Your help in keeping my focus on the Word and not getting distracted by worldly ideas. Thank You, Lord, for hearing and answering this prayer, in Jesus' Name. Amen.

# CHAPTER 9
# THE SPIRIT OF MAMMON

An interesting verse is found in Matthew 6:24, which reads:

> No man can serve two masters: for either he will hate the one, and love the other; or else he will hold to the one, and despise the other. Ye cannot serve God and mammon. (KJV)

As clearly stated in this verse, both God and mammon can each be a master to be served by people, but only one of these will prevail. According to some scholars, mammon is a Syriac word referring to the god of riches that can be worshiped as an idol. This verse is therefore centered on what an individual trusts in, either in the Lord, or in money.

The world is in a financial debt crisis. In the United States as of this writing, consumer debt stands at $16.9 trillion. Consumer debt consists of two components: revolving debt and non-revolving debt. The revolving debt (also called "consumer credit") is mostly credit card debt, and is called "revolving" because the charged balance should be paid off each month. Non-revolving debt consists primarily of loans, specifically auto and student loans. As an aside, home mortgages are considered real estate investment, so that the loan amounts from these financial items are not considered in the non-revolving debt total. The pandemic of 2020 exacerbated some of the components of consumer debt, since the unemployment and reduction in commerce in that period of time caused considerable financial hardships for many persons.

The foregoing information was presented, not to initiate a discussion of debt structure but rather to point out some of the areas in which financial maturity is obviously lacking for most persons. The number of individuals who are debt-free is quite small in comparison to the general population. (Again, the points made in this chapter are centered on the United States, although many persons in other nations are in similar straits). The immediate gratification from offers of "buy now, pay later" continue to lure many people deeper into debt, and the materialism of obtaining things of greed versus things of need likewise continues to drive the crushing financial debt wheel over the lives of significant numbers of consumers.

A wise person once stated that if you want to quickly learn about some individual, watch how they handle money, and to discern even more details about that man or woman, watch how they handle other people's money under their charge. Some adults will "talk a good talk, but not walk a good walk!" So rather than jump into an opinionated monologue about pointing out the financial failings of people, let us embark on an examination of what the Bible has to say concerning money.

First of all, contrary to the opinion of many Christians, the Bible does not condemn money as intrinsically evil. Indeed, we can find the words:

> For the love of money is the root of all evil: which while some coveted after, they have erred from the faith, and pierced themselves through with many sorrows. (1 Tim. 6:10, KJV)

Many a person has sought to accumulate wealth at every chance. The Bible records, "For what is a man profited, if he shall gain the whole world, and lose his own soul? or what shall a man give in exchange for his soul?" (Matt. 16:26, KJV) When incessantly seeking after money occupies the every waking moment of life, seeking after God and His salvation fades into oblivion. Then, when life is over and the accumulated wealth of an individual passes into the hands of someone else, what does the empty soul of that original wealth's owner have to present to the Lord at judgement? Serving the god of money will then be seen for what it really was, namely an idol that drew the person away from eternal life and into the hell of eternal damnation. The covetousness of idolatry (Col. 3: 5) results in serving things rather than the Creator of them!

The conflict of trying to serve God while serving mammon can be clearly delineated with a few examples. So, for instance, the chasing after the "almighty dollar" seven days a week prevents a man or woman from honoring the Sabbath. This is directly contrary to Genesis 20:8-11. The idol of mammon dictates that money must be made on Sunday just as on any other day of the week. The righteousness of the Lord is likewise replaced by "getting over" on whomsoever the idol worshipper may encounter, all for the sake of gain. Relationships, respect for another individual, family time and nurturing of offspring are all left in the dust of running after money. The people or things that stand in the way of incessant monetary pursuit are merely pushed aside. Lastly, the command of "thou shalt have no other gods before me" (Ex. 20:3) pales in comparison to seeking after wealth. There is no seeking after God, no effort spent in pursuing a deepening relationship with Him, and usually no born again salvation experience in those focused purely on monetary gain.

So how does one go about breaking free from the clutches of the idol spirit called mammon? A first step is stated in Romans 12:2, "And be not conformed to this world: but be ye transformed by the renewing of your mind, that ye may prove what is that good, and acceptable, and perfect, will of God" (KJV). In other words, our thinking must be changed so that our behavior will subsequently be changed. Merely attempting to break a bad habit of financial irresponsibility will often lead to the frustration of falling back into old familiar ways. When the Lord becomes a priority, the grip of money on our thinking begins to be destroyed by obeying the command to tithe a tenth of our gross income. The flesh may rebel, one's mind may scream "you fool!" and other such things, but the spirit of mammon's voice in our head will be gradually silenced as our transformed thinking takes over.

The spirit of discontentment presented in Chapter 7 will often join forces with the spirit of mammon to drive an individual into ever-increasingly excessive spending. As our thinking begins to line up with the Word of God, one aspect of our mindset is to practice contentment. The Bible records,

> 6 But godliness with contentment is great gain.
>
> 7 For we brought nothing into this world, and it is certain we can carry nothing out.
>
> 8 And having food and raiment let us be therewith content. (1 Tim. 6:6-8, KJV)

There is nothing at all wrong about desiring to spend money on the things of this world such as a nice house, a beautiful car and attractive clothing. Likewise, there is no problem with investing money in education, training classes, and career preparation endeavors. It is not a failing in financial endeavors to attempt to better oneself, but many persons lose sight of such appropriate goals and instead get caught up in the rat race of worldly pressures such as always obtaining the latest and greatest technological gadgets.

The contentment of godliness is a practiced mindset of gratitude for having the necessities of life without complaining concerning the possessions of others. Indeed, one of the keynote aspects of the contented life is achieved by reaching out to supply that which is needful in the life of someone else. This lifestyle of giving to meet such external needs cannot be achieved when individuals are financially strapped due to excessive spending on themselves as dictated by the spirit of mammon. One person narcissistically quipped, "Get all you can, can all you get, and then sit on the can!" This embodies the world's mindset of ignoring all else, and only looking out for "ole' number one!" The spirit of mammon, however, further runs crosswise of the godliness the Lord desires of each of us in that we cannot be financial givers if we are financial hoarders.

Consider the following verses:

15 If a brother or sister be naked, and destitute of daily food,

16 And one of you say unto them, Depart in peace, be ye warmed and filled; notwithstanding ye give them not those things which are needful to the body; what doth it profit?

17 Even so faith, if it hath not works, is dead, being alone.

18 Yea, a man may say, Thou hast faith, and I have works: shew me thy faith without thy works, and I will shew thee my faith by my works. (James 2:15-18, KJV)

God loves a cheerful giver (2 Cor. 9: 7), because the Lord Himself is a giver (John 3:16). Christians may claim that they have faith, but without some evidence in the natural realm for the same, their faith is dead. Furthermore, the "giving" does not have to be strictly financial, as the above verses indicate that food and/or a warm blanket or coat also qualify. The principle of defeating the spirit of mammon is that of giving out of love, not because of high-pressure fund raising tactics or carefully crafted emotionally charged "sob stories!" Thus, causing our money to obey us in helping others in as much as we are able to do so with a heart set on pleasing the Lord will continue to crush the mammon spirit that has come against us. Indeed, we can read the words, " He that hath a bountiful eye shall be blessed; for he giveth of his bread to the poor" (Pro. 22:9, KJV).

Jesus stated, "The thief cometh not, but for to steal, and to kill, and to destroy: I am come that they might have life, and that they might have it more abundantly" (John 10:10, KJV). The spirit of mammon, on the other hand, seeks only to deceive and destroy, as recorded in First Timothy 6: 9, " But they that will be rich fall into temptation and a snare, and into many foolish and hurtful lusts, which drown men in destruction and perdition" (KJV). The mandate presented to us thus echoes that of Joshua 24:15, "...choose you this day whom ye will serve...but as for me and my house, we will serve the Lord" (KJV).

# Questions for Discussion

1) Why does mammon make a very poor sort of master to serve?

2) Give evidence for a spiritual battle between the Lord and mammon.

3) Why does it require faith to defeat the spirit of mammon?

4) How can the commands of Romans 12:2 aid in the defeat of the spirit of mammon?

5) In what ways do the spending habits of individuals reveal their level of victory over mammon?

# Prayer For Dealing With The Spirit Of Mammon

Heavenly Father, I come in Jesus' Name to declare that I am through with the spirit of mammon. Lord, help me to seek after contentment with freedom from worldly financial pressures. Thank You for helping me to renew my mind with Your Word such that my thoughts line up with Yours, especially where money is concerned. I repent for allowing the idol of materialism to have had such sway in my life in the past. Holy Spirit, help me to follow Your leading in how I handle money and where I spend it. I want my financial life to honor and glorify You in every detail, especially where getting out of debt is concerned. Lord, be magnified in my finances from this day forward, in Jesus' Name I pray. Amen.

# CHAPTER 10
# MENTAL BLINDNESS

A great misconception of many people is that humans see with their eyes, but this is not technically correct. In point of fact, the eyeball is merely a focusing apparatus to display an image on the retina at the rear of said structure. The retina, in turn, is a curved layer of specialized neurons that are light and/or color sensitive. These sensory cells are connected to the occipital lobe of the brain located at the rear of the cranial cavity. It is only here that images which have been focused on the retinas are interpreted in both their spatial and temporal characteristics, or in other words, we "see."

A miraculous instance of proving this can be found in the testimony of Rev. Roscoe Ronald Coyne. At the age of seven, the right eyeball of this fellow was surgically removed. A plastic eyeball was provided to him, but it did not always seem to be positioned appropriately. At any rate, some ten months later during a miracle service conducted by evangelist Daisy Gillock, Ronald Coyne was prayed for and suddenly began to see out of the plastic eyeball. Still more wondrous was the fact that even when he removed the plastic eyeball leaving an empty socket, he could see clearly through that socket! When the left eye was securely covered over with bandages and tape, he could still read from selections of printed material presented to him by many total strangers. He traveled internationally for some forty-three years demonstrating this remarkable ability. (A reference to this can be had at www.johnhamelministries.org/ronald_coyne_testimony.htm). Without question, then, the visual awareness exhibited by this man demonstrates that his brain, not a structural eyeball, was responsible for his miracle vision.

The foregoing information is important in that the Bible points out that the minds of people can be "blinded" from seeing. We can find the words,

3 But if our gospel be hid, it is hid to them that are lost:

4 In whom the god of this world hath blinded the minds of them which believe not, lest the light of the glorious gospel of Christ, who is the image of God, should shine unto them. (2 Cor. 4:3-4, KJV)

In the same way that an individual normally described as "blind" cannot navigate in the natural due to some sort of problem with the visual and/or neural pathways of normally sighted persons, so too, the ability of the mind to see can be blinded by Satan. When this occurs, verse four above states that the light of Jesus is prevented from being clearly perceived in such people. Consequently, they are headed for a godless hell.

It is noteworthy that the persons affected by the god of this world appear to have no other "mental vision" problems, and can thus navigate quite well in the natural world. Indeed, the light of the "glorious gospel of Christ" has been prevented from impacting the mental vision comprehension in these individuals. Anything that obscures light to some degree is described by terms other than "transparent." In this way, a translucent filter will allow some light through, but not all of it. An opaque filter is one that prevents one hundred percent of light from penetrating through its walls, thus producing darkness immediately behind this sort of filter. This description fits well into verse four of the passage just quoted, in that the "light of the glorious gospel of Christ" has been met with a situation of "blindness," (Gr. "opaque" as if smoky; figuratively "obscured"), in their otherwise normally functioning minds.

Unfortunately, the spiritual blindness plaguing both men and women is not relegated to only those outside of the church. Indeed, many wonderful hard-working and church-attending regulars are equally affected, and are thus in no better position than the heathen masses on their way to a godless eternity. How can this be, you may ask? Well, for one plainly stated reason in the verses just quoted, the gospel has not been adequately presented to them. There may be some chronic prejudice against the Word of God, which keeps them from regular church attendance or only allows a token appearance on special occasions such as Easter or Christmas. In addition, the Bible states:

> 3 For the time will come when they will not endure sound doctrine; but after their own lusts shall they heap to themselves teachers, having itching ears;

> 4 And they shall turn away their ears from the truth, and shall be turned unto fables. (2 Tim 4:3-4, KJV)

Sadly, some churches specialize in presenting a religious ceremony every week which is devoid of Bible-based truth. The congregates of these gatherings are either totally in favor of the "same old, same old" drivel (read "sermons") drawn from religious "church-speak" vocabulary, the latest Sunday cartoon page, some poetry, etc. or else they have been duped into thinking that all churches are pretty much the same. In either case, receiving the old fashioned gospel of Jesus and developing an ever-deepening relationship with the Lord is totally foreign to them.

The nefarious nature of mental blindness caused by the god of this world (Satan) is that the persons so affected cannot help themselves out of the situation as a general rule. About the only group of individuals that have any hope of navigating their way out of spiritual blindness is via an experience similar to that of the prodigal son. In the Biblical account found in Luke 15: 11-18, a young man leaves his dad's home to strike out on his own. After ending up out of money, starving, and employed only to feed hogs, the fellow "came to himself" and decided to return home to his father. In the same sort of way, a Christian who is backslidden and without hope in the natural world may have exhausted all of his or her efforts and has "hit bottom" as the expression goes. When such a person "comes to himself," he/she will come back to the Lord and allow the light of the glorious gospel of Jesus to once again direct his or her life.

Unfortunately, however, the vast majority of people attacked by mental blindness do not have the insight to return to the Lord, since they never had a relationship with Him in the first place. Usually, the victim of mental blindness due to Satan's efforts refuses to think of themselves as being blind to the truth, similar to the denial of alcoholics saying that they have no drinking problem or chronic smokers stating that they can quit anytime. Consequently, unless help comes from external sources, those persons refusing admission of Jesus into their lives have sealed their own fate.

There is, nevertheless, a silver lining to this cloud of mental blindness caused by demonic activity obscuring the truth. An example of this will make the point more clear. One minister had prayed many times over a protracted period for one of his siblings to get saved. The brother for whom so much intercession had been made was obviously completely untouched by said extensive prayer efforts. The frustration and disappointment of the praying saint was almost palpable, and with many tears and hours of praying seemingly ineffective, he finally sought the Lord as to why his sibling brother was so resistant to receiving Jesus into his heart. It was then that the Lord revealed two key misconceptions from which this minister was approaching the situation of his brother. First of these was that the minister had no right to impose his will upon the brother, however well meaning the prayers may have been. Thus trying to "force" the brother to get saved was not going to change anything, no matter how many prayers nor how many weeks, months, seasons or years he tried! Secondly, the real problem was not the sibling brother himself, but rather a spirit of mental blindness.

The minister was instructed to exercise the spiritual authority given to every believer, as stated in the following passage of scripture.

9 Wherefore God also hath highly exalted him, and given him a name which is above every name:

10 That at the name of Jesus every knee should bow, of things in heaven, and things in earth, and things under the earth;

11 And that every tongue should confess that Jesus Christ is Lord, to the glory of God the Father. ( Phil 2:9-11, KJV)

The minister was also directed to the passage, "Verily I say unto you, Whatsoever ye shall bind on earth shall be bound in heaven: and whatsoever ye shall loose on earth shall be loosed in heaven" (Matt 18:18, KJV). Lastly, God pointed out the key in Revelation 12:11, "And they overcame him by the blood of the Lamb, and by the word of their testimony..." (KJV).

Now armed with all of this "spiritual ammunition," the minister changed his approach toward getting his brother saved. Rather than an impassioned prayer with tears made to the Lord, the minister dealt with the situation (paraphrased) as follows:

You foul devil of mental blindness, I come against you in the Name of Jesus. This "mental blindness" is just a thing with a name, and at the Name of Jesus, you bow your knee to that Name! It is written that I overcome you by the blood of Jesus, so I plead the blood against you! It is also written, what I bind on Earth is bound in Heaven, and what I loose on Earth is loosed in Heaven. So right now I bind you from my brother _____'s life, and I demand that you loose him and let him go right now, in Jesus' Name! My confession is that he is now free to see his need to receive Jesus into his life. And Heavenly Father, I thank you that the assignment of that devil called "mental blindness" is broken off of my brother, and that I will get the report that he is saved, in Jesus' Name, Amen!

Many months and even years of intercessory prayer for this minister's brother had not effected any change, but reportedly within three weeks after using this "spiritual ammunition" attack against the demonic cause of the problem, that brother phoned and said he had gotten saved! It is a foregone conclusion that many persons would likewise get saved if Christians would exercise their God-given authority against those agents from the kingdom of darkness called "mental blindness" and let the Word of God fight for them!

# Questions For Discussion

1) Why is it unlikely that persons attacked by mental blindness can free themselves from it?

2) Since Jesus is the Light of the world, how is it that even some churchgoers cannot see that light?

3) Explain how a legally blind person could simultaneously have no mental blindness.

4) How can merely altering the manner in which we pray help regarding unsaved loved ones?

5) What is a common denominator between alcoholics and mental blindness?

# Prayer For Dealing With Mental Blindness

Heavenly Father, thank You for helping me to understand what mental blindness has done in my life. Right now I plead the blood of Jesus over my spiritual eyes that I may clearly discern the truths of Your Word. Help me, Lord, like the prodigal son individual to have come to my senses and returned to You with my whole heart. Forgive me, Father, for past religious unbelief. May the words of my mouth and the meditations of my heart be acceptable in Your sight, my strength and my redeemer. In Jesus' Name I pray. Amen.

# CHAPTER 11
# COMPROMISE

In the book of James, chapter five, we can find the words:

> 12 But above all things, my brethren, swear not, neither by heaven, neither by the earth, neither by any other oath: but let your yea be yea; and your nay, nay; lest ye fall into condemnation. (James 5:12, KJV)

The act of swearing an oath on some recognized institution or divine personality has been commonly performed for centuries in order to make one's words appear to be above reproach or categorically truthful. The verse quoted above, however, gives another admonition to believers to remain steadfast in either their affirmation or denial of some matter. Maintaining an undeviating position on a moral stand is stated as a mandatory character trait for Christians.

The worldly views of morality can be roughly grouped into one of two categories: situational ethics and moral relativism. Briefly, moral relativism is a philosophical stance that declares there really is no true "right" or "wrong." In this way, an individual making a decision is held to have been neither in the right nor in the wrong regarding the circumstances of the results from said decision. Situational ethics, on the other hand, maintains that there is definitely a "right" or "wrong," but this is totally dependent upon the circumstances in the context of the decision. In this latter point of view, the same decision in two totally different sets of environmental elements could be totally "right" in one of these, and totally "wrong" in the other!

The Bible declares that wavering from one position of moral correctness to another is not to be found in the lives of believers. A classic situation of this sort can be found in the words:

21 And Elijah came unto all the people, and said, How long
halt ye between two opinions? if the Lord be God, follow
him: but if Baal, then follow him. And the people answered
him not a word. (1 Kings 18:21, KJV)

Quite literally, a compromise between following the Lord or
seeking after demonic worship represents a difference of choosing life
or death. The problem resulting from compromising one's focus
particularly in regards to worship is that it violates the clearest
teachings from the Bible for a believer.

4 Hear, O Israel: The Lord our God is one Lord:

5 And thou shalt love the Lord thy God with all thine heart,
and with all thy soul, and with all thy might. (Deut. 6:4-5,
KJV)

Indeed, a person cannot worship and serve the Lord with all the
heart, soul and mind and simultaneously hold a place of reverence for
an idol deity. This would present an untenable conflict of remaining
single-minded versus being "double minded." The scriptures declare, "
A double minded man is unstable in all his ways," ( Jas. 1:8, KJV), and
again, "Draw nigh to God, and he will draw nigh to you. Cleanse your
hands, ye sinners; and purify your hearts, ye double minded" (Jas. 4:8,
KJV). This concept of having a pure heart before the Lord is crucial for
believers. In fact, the Bible declares, " Whereas the object and purpose
of our instruction and charge is love, which springs from a pure heart
and a good (clear) conscience and sincere (unfeigned) faith," (1 Tim.
1:5, AMP).

Much can be said regarding an individual having a "sincere" or
"unfeigned" faith. For instance, the root meaning of the word "sincere"
comes from two Latin words: *"sine"* (without) and *"cera"* (wax).
Literally, then, the two particles of this word render "sincere" as

meaning "without wax." In Biblical times, marble artisans sometimes covered up imperfections in statues and other works of art by applying wax to the stone. Some of these sculptors even had two bins of artwork for sale in their marketplace shop. One of these was designated "sincereus" (without wax) and the other was "insincere" (with wax). Pottery makers also filled in cracks with wax, then painted over the imperfections. While these practices might seem relatively harmless, more ominously, unscrupulous brick layers would sometimes use wax, rather than more expensive cement, and when it melted in the hot Middle Eastern sun, bricks could shift and structures collapse causing injury and death. The guarantee of "sine cera" was therefore an important claim!

Imagine, if you will, a housewife purchasing an item of pottery for home use, only to find that the walls of the vessel were compromised by wax at one or more places rendering the container useless. In fact, one method of testing the integrity of just such pottery was to pour hot water on it. This would cause any wax present to melt, and thus reveal the flaws in the vessel. Still more interestingly, another meaning of "sincere" is "judged by sunlight." Here again, the hot Middle Eastern sunlight could soften and then melt wax of "insincere" items, and their true nature be revealed. Extrapolate this last train of thought to the lives of contemporary churchgoers. If the "Son-light" of Jesus is focused on their lives, will there be the "wax" of compromise melted away to reveal flaws formerly covered up?

Developing this concept of "wax-y Christians" still further we can read, "Beloved, think it not strange concerning the fiery trial which is to try you, as though some strange thing happened unto you" (1 Peter 4:12, KJV). Persecution comes to all Christians, and while not all events qualify as "fire" per se, a common expression for the hardships faced by some persons is that they are "going through the fire." Whereas many individuals may claim to be stalwart and strong people, when pressured by situations that extend beyond their comfort zone and/

or expected circumstances, the true nature of the person will often be revealed. Sometimes, weaknesses of which the man or woman were totally unaware are brought to the surface, and they are jarred into realizing that change is needed in their character. As they seek the Lord's help in dealing with the now-revealed flaw, they can eliminate both it and the need for waxy cover-up. Thus when the fiery trial is over, the person will come out better and more experienced than was previously the case.

A perfect example of a true fiery trial is the Biblical account of Shadrach, Meshach, and Abednego found in Daniel chapter three. To summarize that event, the evil king Nebuchadnezzar had a golden image made, and required all persons to bow down to it when some musicians played their music. The three Hebrew young men refused to comply with the king's order, and this infuriated the evil king. He threatened to have them cremated alive in an open furnace, but they still would not compromise their unwillingness to worship the golden image. Nebuchadnezzar then ordered the furnace heated seven times more than the usual fire, and for the three Hebrew captives to be thrown into the same. We can pick up the account from that point.

20 And he commanded the most mighty men that were in his army to bind Shadrach, Meshach, and Abed-nego, and to cast them into the burning fiery furnace.

21 Then these men were bound in their coats, their hosen, and their hats, and their other garments, and were cast into the midst of the burning fiery furnace.

22 Therefore because the king's commandment was urgent, and the furnace exceeding hot, the flame of the fire slew those men that took up Shadrach, Meshach, and Abed-nego.

23 And these three men, Shadrach, Meshach, and Abed-nego, fell down bound into the midst of the burning fiery furnace.

24 Then Nebuchadnezzar the king was astonied, and rose up in haste, and spake, and said unto his counsellors, Did not we cast three men bound into the midst of the fire? They answered and said unto the king, True, O king.

25 He answered and said, Lo, I see four men loose, walking in the midst of the fire, and they have no hurt; and the form of the fourth is like the Son of God.

26 Then Nebuchadnezzar came near to the mouth of the burning fiery furnace, and spake, and said, Shadrach, Meshach, and Abed-nego, ye servants of the most high God, come forth, and come hither. Then Shadrach, Meshach, and Abed-nego, came forth of the midst of the fire.

27 And the princes, governors, and captains, and the king's counsellors, being gathered together, saw these men, upon whose bodies the fire had no power, nor was an hair of their head singed, neither were their coats changed, nor the smell of fire had passed on them. (Dan 3:20-27, KJV)

The text of the passage reveals that God honored the non-compromising stand of Shadrach, Meshach, and Abednego. Indeed, Jesus Himself showed up in the midst of the flames with those young men and was walking around in the fire with them! Careful reading of this text also brings out many details that are easy to otherwise miss. So, for instance, the smell of fire was not detected on the clothing of these young men when they emerged from the furnace. Anyone who has been around a campfire for virtually any length of time knows full well that the smell of the smoke from fiery embers adheres to their hair and clothing very strongly. Nevertheless, these three Hebrew men were without odors of a fire when emerging from the furnace conflagration.

The text also reveals another wonderful miracle in the fiery furnace. The flames had been increased to such an extent that the army strongmen who cast the Hebrew fellows into the furnace were slain by the intense heat. When they were thrown into the fire, Shadrach, Meshach, and Abednego were bound, but when commanded by king Nebuchadnezzar to come out of the same, they were able to walk out freely. In other words, all the fiery trial really accomplished was to burn off the ropes binding the Hebrew young men and setting them free! So too, when a contemporary Christian goes through a fiery trial, as he or she exits the other side of the situation, they find that they have been set at liberty from bondage that formerly held them! In a word, a "test" brings a "testimony!"

The words of Joshua 24:15 find special significance here for those persons tempted to compromise their faith: "...choose you this day whom ye will serve... but as for me and my house, we will serve the Lord" (KJV). Are they one of those individuals (Matt. 15:8) who honors Him with their lips, but their heart is far from the Lord? On the other hand, are they "*sine cira*" and thus without wax such that they have a pure heart and an uncompromising stand on the Word of God? The apostle Paul even stated, "I am amazed that you are so quickly deserting Him who called you by the grace of Christ, for a different gospel; which is really not another; only there are some who are disturbing you and want to distort the gospel of Christ" (Romans 13:14, KJV). Compromising the truth of the Word of God to include traditions/eclectic-sounding religious man-made beliefs and so on can only be considered a distorted gospel. As believers, we must be single-minded and not double-minded, always prepared to stand against compromise.

# Questions For Discussion

1) How is a Christian-based stand for morality different from worldly morality?

2) What was the main point made concerning being a sincere Christian?

3) Discuss how fiery trials can reveal the level of sincerity in Christians.

4) Explain how compromise can result in the practice of idolatry.

# Prayer For Dealing With Compromise

Heavenly Father, I come in Jesus' Name to pray for Your help in resisting compromise. I don't want to be a double-minded person who follows some distorted version of the gospel. Help me, Lord, to be a believer with a pure heart toward You, and not someone who vacillates depending upon the situations I encounter. Thank You, Holy Spirit, for opening my spiritual eyes to clearly discern where the light of Your Word is leading me and following that path. I ask this in the Name of Jesus. Amen.

# CHAPTER 12
# UNTHANKFULNESS

A stark prophetic warning for contemporary Christians is written in the following passage from Second Timothy, chapter three.

1 This know also, that in the last days perilous times shall come.

2 For men shall be lovers of their own selves, covetous, boasters, proud, blasphemers, disobedient to parents, unthankful, unholy,

3 Without natural affection, trucebreakers, false accusers, incontinent, fierce, despisers of those that are good,

4 Traitors, heady, highminded, lovers of pleasures more than lovers of God; (2 Tim 3:1-4, KJV)

While many teachings could be derived from the passage just quoted, the character flaw to be dealt with in this chapter is that of being "unthankful." In this period of demanded entitlement, so many worldly persons have come to develop a mindset that they are owed various blessings merely because they are taking up space and using up oxygen on planet Earth! Consequently, there is no perceived need for an expression of gratitude. Tragically, this same mentality has invaded the church, and many persons in various congregations fill the chairs and pews with hearts and minds embedded in "self."

The Bible sums up all such worldly mindsets in the following passage of scripture:

15 Love not the world, neither the things that are in the world. If any man love the world, the love of the Father is not in him.

16 For all that is in the world, the lust of the flesh, and the lust of the eyes, and the pride of life, is not of the Father, but is of the world. (1 John 2:15-16, KJV)

So what is it that makes being thankful such a difficult commodity to be had in the lives of contemporary Christians? Where has the disconnection occurred between love for God and His goodness versus expressions of heartfelt gratitude for the same in the lives of believers? As stated in the verses from Second Timothy at the outset of this chapter, there are various facets of "lovers of pleasures more than lovers of God" that can be identified as contributing to an ungrateful mentality. Nevertheless, herein is presented the additional factor of "judgment."

The Bible commands that a man not think more highly of himself than he ought to think (Rom. 12:3), and coincident with this is to not judge himself better than his brother by despising and criticizing him. In biblical times, there was much hatred between the Jews and Gentiles, so much so that they were often not even on speaking terms. Consequently, when Jesus Himself attempted to have a conversation with the Samaritan woman at the well of Sychar, He was met with suspicion because "the Jews have no dealings with the Samaritans," (John 4:9, KJV). Even within the Hebrew community there was denigration of fellow Jews by members of the Pharisees. A classic instance of this was presented in the account of Jesus having healed the man born blind.

29 We know that God spake unto Moses: as for this fellow, we know not from whence he is.

30 The man answered and said unto them, Why herein is a marvellous thing, that ye know not from whence he is, and yet he hath opened mine eyes.

31 Now we know that God heareth not sinners: but if any man be a worshipper of God, and doeth his will, him he heareth.

32 Since the world began was it not heard that any man opened the eyes of one that was born blind.

33 If this man were not of God, he could do nothing.

34 They answered and said unto him, Thou wast altogether born in sins, and dost thou teach us? And they cast him out. (John 9:29-34, KJV)

Obviously, the Pharisees were not at all pleased or celebrating the healing of this formerly blind individual, let alone not giving thanks for his healing. Still worse, that fact that the newly sighted fellow was in the temple testifying about a man of God the Jewish leadership did not recognize aroused both anger and religious judgment. Suffice it to state that many of the judgmental attitudes presented in the New Testament deal with religious prejudice between the Jews and Gentiles, and even factions within the Jewish leadership. Equally significant, however, are accounts of the disciples judging others, as in the following verses.

1 And as Jesus passed by, he saw a man which was blind from his birth.

2 And his disciples asked him, saying, Master, who did sin, this man, or his parents, that he was born blind?

3 Jesus answered, Neither hath this man sinned, nor his parents: but that the works of God should be made manifest in him. (John 9:1-3, KJV)

Without provocation, the immediate response from the disciples was to assign blame for the visual defect in this fellow. The depth of their inculcated judgmental attitude was clearly betrayed by their question about sin by the man born blind. How was this person supposed to have sinned *in utero?* Jesus dismissed both that possibility, and the belief of "transmutation of souls" held by the Jews, (in which sins of a previous life were dealt with by afflictions in the life of a subsequent individual), when He said "neither." The Lord could have easily launched into an explanation of death entering the world by the sin of Adam (later stated in Rom. 12:5), but instead exhibited compassion on the man and manifested healing for his eyes with clay. The principle in this passage of scripture for us today is not to be so quick to act in judgment but rather to act in compassion for the needs of others. We will then have cause to give thanks to God for the healings and deliverances manifested in the lives of those to whom we minister.

Judgment can also derive from envy of some aspect in the lives of others. So for instance, a neighbor has obtained a new car that far exceeds the value of the one we drive, causing some to criticize the aforesaid new vehicle. Emphasis on the other person's possessions negates giving thanks that we have our own means of transportation. A sense of superiority in socioeconomic position can many times result in a judgmental and condescending view of others. This may take the form of "Well, they aren't any more deserving than I am!" Some persons may even go so far as to denigrate others in saying, "They aren't worthy to have received that gift." This latter comment often being made in the face of no need of the same by the critic, yet greatly needed by the recipient person. The additional elements of both anger and/or pride about someone else's blessings only further reduce the chances of thanksgiving in the life of the critic. The list of the possibilities for such judgmental attitudes is virtually inexhaustible.

Finally, there is considerable harm done in the personal life of an unthankful person because their attitude will completely short-circuit their prayer life. We can find the words:

> 6 Have no anxiety about anything, but in everything by
> prayer and supplication with thanksgiving let your requests
> be made known to God. (Phil 4:6-7, RSV)

We literally cannot follow the dictates of the Word of God to give thanks for our prayers having been answered as per Mark 11:24 if we are of the mindset that there is no cause for thanks until we see manifestations of the desired result. This bears more significant attention, so let us look carefully at the verse from Mark chapter eleven.

> 24 Therefore I say unto you, What things soever ye desire,
> when ye pray, believe that ye receive them, and ye shall have
> them. (KJV)

Notice that the admonition for answered petition prayer is to believe that you have received the desired answer while you are stating the prayer to the Lord. The giving of thanks is thus a statement of faith to God that you believe He has heard your prayer and answered the same. Consider the words from Hebrews 11:1, "Now faith is the substance of things hoped for, the evidence of things not seen" (KJV). In other words, our faith stands as the evidence for the answer to our prayers not yet seen. Consequently, we can demonstrate one of the "works of faith" by giving the Lord thanks for the same. Indeed, James 2:17 plainly states: "Even so faith, if it hath not works, is dead, being alone" (KJV). By our giving voice to our faith and believing that God has granted the answer to our prayer, our giving of thanks for that answer can be seen to be critically important.

The association of a thankful attitude and a successful prayer life cannot be overly stated. Indeed, there is herein one of Satan's primary reasons for fomenting ungrateful mindsets in Christians. If we are mired in a grumpy mental cesspool consisting of a plethora of reasons for not being thankful for things in our lives, Satan knows that this lack of gratitude and subsequent lack of answered prayer will most certainly stymie any desire to pray in the first place. Unthankfulness thus becomes a spiritual weapon from the kingdom of darkness against the church!

Thanklessness is furthermore a violation of scriptural commands for the everyday lives of Christians beyond merely dealing with praying. The following scriptures illustrate this important concept.

Col. 3:17

And whatsoever ye do in word or deed, do all in the name of the Lord Jesus, giving thanks to God and the Father by him. (KJV)

Heb. 13:15

By him therefore let us offer the sacrifice of praise to God continually, that is, the fruit of our lips giving thanks to his name. (KJV)

Col. 2:6-7

6 As therefore you received Christ Jesus the Lord, so live in him,

7 rooted and built up in him and established in the faith, just as you were taught, abounding in thanksgiving. (RSV)

1 Thess. 5:18

In every thing give thanks: for this is the will of God in Christ Jesus concerning you. (KJV)

That last scripture cited from First Thessalonians 5:18 bears some additional clarification. The admonition appears to imply giving of thanks "in every thing." This cannot possibly mean we are to give God thanks for cancer, heart attacks, children dying at a young age, etc. because these are not the works of the Lord. Satan is the one who comes only to steal, kill, and destroy. Therefore, the giving of thanks "in every thing" must carry with it the meaning of giving praise, worship and thanks to God for His goodness and His Love despite what the current circumstances of our lives may be. Indeed, "For we walk by faith, not by sight" (2 Cor. 5:7, KJV). Emotionally and logically it may be difficult to give God thanks and praise in the midst of trying circumstances, but this is the essence of the verse: "By him therefore let us offer the sacrifice of praise to God continually, that is, the fruit of our lips giving thanks to his name" (Heb 13:15, KJV). The giving of thanks in these situations is thus a true sacrifice on our part to the Lord. Unthankfulness thus diminishes our ministry to the Lord as well as short-circuiting our own faith life and success as Christians. Let us begin today to cultivate a thankful lifestyle as a parameter of vibrant faith!

# Questions For Discussion

1. Why is emphasis on "self" such an enemy of thankfulness?
2. Explain how being unthankful can be an effective weapon of Satan.
3. How do anger and pride often reduce or negate thankfulness in our lives?

4. How are our prayers and our thought life related concerning getting answers from God?

5. How does judging others potentially affect our walk of faith?

# Prayer For Dealing With Unthankfulness

Heavenly Father, I come in Jesus' Name to ask forgiveness for my unthankful attitudes. I have so much for which to thank You, and I can see now why many of my prayers have been hindered. Holy Spirit, move now in my life to make me aware of the blessings that are mine to have every day and to be thankful for them! Let me begin right now by thanking You for Jesus in my heart. I don't want to be a thankless person anymore, so Lord, help me to renew my mind with Your Word so that being thankful is a part of my everyday life. In Jesus' Name I pray. Amen.

# CHAPTER 13
# FINAL THOUGHTS

For many persons, a book centered on dealing with the kingdom of darkness and its minions is hardly the sort of preferred reading material they would at first glance prioritize in their lives. Indeed, the spiritual subject matter herein at its essence is one of negativity, not positivity. Nevertheless, much is to be gained by those individuals who refuse to live in denial of demonic forces and their activities. The vast majority of the unsaved natural populace simply wants to avoid having to deal with an invisible dimension concerning their existence. These latter people are stuck in an endless struggle of attempting to explain much of the evil existing in our society as merely the result of "bad people" who have done "bad things."

The import of the topics presented in this book centers on creating an awareness in its readers that there is a direct connection between the activities of the invisible spiritual realm and the natural realm. The Bible uses the term "carnal" to describe men and women who are led around only by their five physical senses. As such, then, when only input from the natural world around us is allowed into their thinking, "denial" is a significant aspect of their real-world mindset where the "facts" don't line up with many of the situations encountered.

However, instead of the childish repetition of the question "Why?" to every incident that does not align with carnal understanding, many Christians have come to the awareness of a spiritual realm that explains much of what the natural realm cannot hope to comprehend. Indeed, those who are led by the Spirit of the living God perceive things that go far beyond classroom learning, psychological analysis, scientific instrumentation investigation, and such like. These individuals are able to discern that which the carnal person cannot hope to grasp. The Bible even goes so far as to state:

12 Now we have received, not the spirit of the world, but the spirit which is of God; that we might know the things that are freely given to us of God.

13 Which things also we speak, not in the words which man's wisdom teacheth, but which the Holy Ghost teacheth; comparing spiritual things with spiritual.

14 But the natural man receiveth not the things of the Spirit of God: for they are foolishness unto him: neither can he know them, because they are spiritually discerned. (1 Cor. 2:12-14, KJV)

Hopefully, the topics explored in this book have brought a heightened awareness and understanding of some of the specific nefarious agents with which we all have to deal. Nevertheless, the reader of this book could have ploughed through the pages from front cover to the back, and still come away with little to have been gained despite a genuine sincerity coupled with church attendance. The problem in cases such as this is simply that the reader needs to ask Jesus to come into his or her heart and be born-again in their spirit-man. The easy and simple way to step into this new spiritual life can be seen in the following scriptures.

9 That if thou shalt confess with thy mouth the Lord Jesus, and shalt believe in thine heart that God hath raised him from the dead, thou shalt be saved.

10 For with the heart man believeth unto righteousness; and with the mouth confession is made unto salvation Rom. 10:9-10, KJV)

The significant points in those latter verses are that you, the reader, must believe those things in your heart, not just your head, and secondly that you must SAY them to the Lord, not just think them in your head! When this has been done, be prepared dear reader, for both the Bible to begin making more meaningful sense to you, and spiritual understanding of many of the situations in the lives of folks to become clearer. Welcome to the family of the Lord!

# ADDENDUM

If you have enjoyed reading this book, another print volume by this author is available in many bookstores:

**Who is the Bride of Christ? Hint: It's Not Who You Think!**

www.ingramcontent.com/pod-product-compliance
Lightning Source LLC
Chambersburg PA
CBHW031426130726
47989CB00003B/1044